THE MONOGRAPH SERIES OF
THE PSYCHOANALYTIC STUDY OF THE CHILD

Monograph No. 3

SELECTED PROBLEMS OF ADOLESCENCE

With Special Emphasis on Group Formation

THE PSYCHOANALYTIC STUDY OF THE CHILD
MONOGRAPH NO. 3

Selected Problems
of Adolescence

With Special Emphasis on Group Formation

By

HELENE DEUTSCH, M.D.

INTERNATIONAL UNIVERSITIES PRESS, INC.

NEW YORK

THE MONOGRAPH SERIES OF
THE PSYCHOANALYTIC STUDY OF THE CHILD

CONTENTS

SELECTED PROBLEMS OF ADOLESCENCE

With Special Emphasis on Group Formation

CHAPTER 1

PSYCHOLOGICAL PROBLEMS OF ADOLESCENCE

The leading theme in adolescence is the conflict between generations. This conflict, posed in terms of a definite age period, did at one time seem to reflect an accurate conception by adolescents of adult identity and maturity. For the contemporary adolescent, however, that concept seems no longer to exist in its strict definition. Quite the contrary: many adolescents are troubled by the fact that the image of the "mature" generation of their parents becomes somewhat obscured for them, once they discover that parents themselves are often still involved in their own, not yet completed adolescence.[1] The tolerance of the parents, their gesture of being mature yet understanding, is then seen as only a role, which conceals an actual co-acting *at the same level with* their children. The parents are apparently not aware that, in giving their children freedom and independence, they are pushing them out at a time when these children are still in need of parental guidance and protection. Experience seems to prove that it is better for growing youth that their attempts to achieve freedom, along with their aggressive protest against authority, should first be begun at home and only later on taken up in the larger field that is now the arena of adolescent

[1] Therese Benedek (1959) regards parenthood as a developmental stage. Evidently, many parents of today's adolescents do not reach that stage.

9

"revolution." This is especially true of girls and their so-
called "sexual freedom."[2]

The literature about the psychological problems of adolescence increased greatly during the last decade, along the lines
of two fundamentally different approaches: one lays its stress
on the more individual aspect of the problem, as in psychoanalysis; the other regards the individual adolescent as a
member of society, and considers his actions, his problems,
even his aspirations to be the resultants of forces that have
their origin in social developments.

The dichotomy between these two points of view, however, no longer holds, as it did earlier. In the sociological
literature, the application of a psychoanalytic orientation has
revealed itself to be more and more fruitful and therefore
more and more necessary; on the other hand, sociology, as a
significant aspect of the study of human behavior, has been
finding its way into the field of psychology, and particularly
into psychoanalysis (Hartmann, 1944).

My own interest in adolescence was reawakened by events
outside the sphere of the psychoanalytic couch. It was revived
by the "noise from the street," so to speak, the increasingly
evident restlessness of adolescents, which has more and more
come to be expressed not so much in individualistic forms as
in group formations. On looking for ways to approach this
problem, I discovered that it was necessary to consult the
sociologists and their work. The vast increase in as well as
the differentiation of sociological literature during the recent
past had made my previous knowledge of sociology of relatively limited usefulness. In attempting to apply sociology to
the problems of adolescence, however, I have had to focus
specifically on some aspects of these problems and to elim-
inate others from consideration.

For an observer who has had the privilege of witnessing
events under three different sociocultural conditions, it is a

[2] See Chapter 4 on the adolescence of girls.

truly fascinating experience to try to determine the degree to which differences in external conditions actually do influence adolescent individuals, particularly in the formation of their social groups, which are generally built up on the basis of identity of physiological development. The tendency of adolescents to such group formations makes them, according to the sociologists, members of a subculture, with definite social rights and obligations.

The question of whether the adolescent of our times has psychological problems that are different from those faced by his counterpart two and three generations earlier, as well as to what extent his expression of these problems has changed with the social structure of his society—a question such as this must be answered from both sides: from that of the psychologist and that of the sociologist.

Modern sociologists say that, in addition to the customary personal problems of the adolescent, there now exists something that they call "youth problems." Some are of the opinion that, in American society at present, there is no incentive for the younger generation to take part in social developments. The goals of the grownups are distrusted or rejected by them, and contemporary social-political aims in general do not seem to them to present ideas that are capable of fulfilling their emotional and intellectual needs.

Only in small minorities do the young—most specifically, the students— find their allegiance: they wish to collaborate not with members of the adult group, nor with those of the ruling class, but rather with organizations whose goals are in opposition to those of "authority," "order," the "system." Yet participation in the civil rights movement and in antiwar activities, as well as the expression of sympathy, at least in words, with revolutionary activities in other countries—all this is apparently not enough to make any significant portion of the younger generation a real part of current social upheavals.

It is true that American adolescents have their own "youth

problems," of a highly personal, individual character. The absence of participation on their part in larger political movements is in part due to the fact that they do not find in the affluent society aims that can appeal to them. On the other hand, they observe that students in other countries, as well as in all revolutionary-progressive political movements of the past, have themselves been leaders, either in bringing these movements to life or else by joining already existent and active groups. The chief reasons for the negative attitude among American youth thus seem to be: *first,* the comparative absence of revolutionary-progressive ideologies from contemporary American society; and *second,* their own intensive, prolonged, and competitive process of schooling, which to a great extent effectively separates young men and women from the older generation and thus blocks them off from exercising any direct influence on the sociopolitical situation.

As a result, we are now confronted, particularly in the United States, with a new picture of public life. Youths now tend to create social groups of their own, which try to fulfill *their* wishes and goals, "undefiled by adult contamination," and even to impose these goals on the majority of their elders. They have their own music, dances, theater, books, as well as their leaders, their ideal heroes—and their forms of delinquency. It is only as individuals that they either join more conservative political groups, as recognized units of big organizations (Young Democrats, Young Republicans), or become a part of existing groups of protest.

Whatever youth and its organizations want and fight for, it is now certain to set them against the older generation and its demands; it is at bottom a protest, a "revolution" against the established social order. Observations by the sociologists have suggested that, for the developmental processes of present-day adolescents, it is psychologically not decisive whether the direction of their political efforts is toward the Left or the Right. In both instances, those efforts are intended to serve positive goals, and in either case, they may or may not be successful. The overall effect of the individual emancipation that is sought by youth in its rebellion and protest can be, in a sense, achieved with a politically conservative or even a reactionary orientation (Schiff, 1964). We need, therefore, to examine more closely the dynamic forces behind these various forms of acting upon reality and to bring our findings into closer relationship with the psychological developmental processes of individual adolescents.

As a whole, psychoanalytic insight into the dynamic forces of adolescent group formations reveals the identity of these forces with those that are involved in the more individual and purely personal problems typical of adolescence. Numerous observations on adolescents have shown that at one time one component of the inner struggle has the greatest impact on the adolescent's personality, at another time another component. The same thing can be observed with regard to adolescent group formations: they too are formed under the impact of inner forces, which give a specific character to the group. The expression of internal problems is, of course, also conditioned, and in a double way, by society: first, by the society at large in which youth lives and acts; second, by the attitude of their childhood society, their family environment. The remote generation—the grandparents with *their* ideals and the influences of *their* social milieu—may still, via the parents as well as directly, influence the psychological make-up of our contemporary youth. Psychoanalysis with its emphasis on inner events cannot deny, and has never attempted to deny, the role of sociological influences.

The goal of this study is to develop psychoanalytic insight into the origin, nature, and goals of the group formations of our contemporary adolescents. I recognized early that, with this kind of approach, I would have to know individually as many young people as possible, in order to be able to understand their psychology as members of groups.

The extension of educational goals and the fact that society now permits the youths to postpone to a later age[3] their taking on the responsibilities of grownups—and even encourages them to do so—has also lengthened the period of adolescence, and made a new terminology necessary. One speaks today of "teen-agers" (early adolescence), and refers to only the older adolescents as "youth." In this monograph, I shall call the majority of the objects of my observations "late adolescents," in that their problems are still really those of adolescents, while their status in the community is at the same time that of maturing (by contrast with "grownups," they are often referred to, in academic and other circles, as "young adults").

DESCRIPTION OF APPROACH

Before reporting my observations, I should like to say a few words about the methodology employed in this work. First, it seemed important for my project to see these young people on their own initiative, rather than as the result of professional referral. The latter usually results in confrontation with neurotically sick individuals, who are in need of prolonged therapy.

I have the impression that I have succeeded in reaping, out of my retirement from all participation in public and academic activities, a great advantage. To the young people who have consulted me during these last years, I have been an old woman who could be trusted to be at least neutral, since she is not burdened by the demands of professional prestige. They have come to me on the basis of hearsay, influenced by my reputation in those places in which students gather by themselves. Dormitories in particular create an atmopshere of intimacy and confidence; there the conversations are not always solely about school and intellectual topics, but often have a more personal character, so that secret worries are exchanged. This has led more and more often to students' recommending therapy—and me. The fact that I am not con-

3 This is a general truth, the impact on which of military draft revision still remains to be seen.

nected in any way with their college has been very much in my favor.

Since these gatherings include both boys and girls, my patients are of either sex. Their intellectual level is usually in keeping with the demands of their school and, in so far as the majority are in college, the interests that they share are more or less advanced.

I do not ask their names, etc. Sometimes they speak about school, and sometimes about their families—especially in cases in which there is a manifest conflict. I merely ask them not to report our interviews to their family (thereby reversing the assurance we usually give patients in this regard).

Some—especially girls—start by referring to my writings; some open, "Last month I had a dream." They evidently want to cover their embarrassment by speaking "analytically" at once, but it takes a very short time for real contact to be established between us. The second interview is usually already in the spirit of a very good collaboration.

The composition of this group is very striking. I do not see really sick adolescents: only twice have I directed a patient to somebody else for treatment; once I had to obtain the permission of a mentally very sick student to contact his parents. I see very few students from Harvard or Radcliffe. Much work is being done with them, I know, and I do not want to interfere in it. Boston provides the opportunity, however, to see college students who come from various social groups and whose goals reflect—either positively or negatively—the social standing of their families. I was fascinated to learn how few actual differences there are in their psychological problems, despite the differences in their intellectual level and future ambitions.

The problems usually have to do with an acute situation: examinations have to be taken, or decisions made about "majors"; sometimes an affair must be helped to continue or else to be given up. And there are even more complicated situations. In the main, however, these young people come because of their awareness that their difficulties are not solely external or realistic.

In dealing with these adolescents, I have been guided by an approach that has begun to be something of a neglected art in psychoanalytic treatment. I put great emphasis on empathy, which helps the analyst to detect, often as early as in the preliminary contacts with the patient, the latter's unconscious secrets—before he (or she) has learned how to guard them better. On the other hand, the intuitive understanding that these adolescents themselves display can then be utilized for the solution of their acute problems, generally within a short time. It is a mutually constructive and gratifying experience—for them and for me. The patients become—at least the majority of them—able to function more rationally, while I have learned much about the problems of adolescents and about their activities.

Intuitive as this approach may be, it has had to rest on a certain methodology, which I want to indicate briefly. For a psychoanalyst, every therapeutic approach is based on what is already known analytically about the psychic functions, mechanisms, etc., and above all, on his own clinical experiences. In my case, these experiences had been acquired during many years of analytic practice.

In my work with adolescents, I was confronted with a great variety of the intrapsychic difficulties that are typical for this period of life. In some, there was a sudden influx of instinctual forces; in others, reality demands that surpassed their capacity (which was often purely intellectual); in still others, increased superego demands, coupled with strong reactions of guilt, etc.

In my interviews, I avoid—especially at the beginning—any psychoanalytic interpretation. Many of the young and intelligent patients have already had some orientation in psychoanalysis, and they come prepared to oppose analysis, to accept it enthusiastically, or at least to engage in discussion about it. All these I refuse to go along with. I offer an interpretation only when I feel certain that it will reinforce collaboration and not resistance. What I lay stress on, as a rule, is the recent problem; the infantile situation is seldom revived.

Very often I have the opportunity to see students who are full of misunderstanding, yet quite eager to involve the therapist in argumentation, frequently of an obsessional character. At such times it is difficult to restrain one's irritation; nevertheless, one must keep in mind the increase of narcissistic vulnerability during adolescence and proceed very tactfully, for narcissistic trauma is quite often the main problem of adolescent patients (this was especially true of my men patients). Intellectual defenses quickly fall, and when the therapist comments that he (or she) can be helpful only if the patient is helping, it is amazing how rapidly the therapeutic alliance is established. The whole situation evidently captures the imagination of these young people, so that the alliance is generally quite warm and sincere. Seldom have I encountered mistrust or unwillingness to collaborate. Upon being questioned by these young people about the reason for my interest in them, I offer a sincere answer, along with the assurance of my being absolutely discreet. Only twice has a patient canceled all visits beyond the first interview.

Generally speaking, the boys have been more eager to speak (spontaneously) about their interest in sociopolitical problems, their evaluation of public figures, and their refusal (or desire) to participate in group activities. The reasons that brought them to my office were commonly in the intellectual sphere: learning difficulties, problems with teachers, the paralyzing anxiety of competition, etc. Seldom were love and sexuality the topics of our conversations.

The girls' interests were divided: highly intellectual aspirations, striving for achievement, great competitive ambitions were present here too; but, as compared with their male colleagues, only for the minority. Their interests and problems were manifestly (or unconsciously) of a more emotional, erotic nature. Two case histories, which are presented in Chapter 4, will provide us with more insight into the methodology, and also show that contemporary girls are often involved in problems that are not very different from those of their grandmother's generation.

Speaking of grandmothers, I do not underestimate the fact that the most helpful factor in the therapeutic situation was a kind of "grandmother transference." It is interesting to see the adolescents reviving their positive childhood relationship to grandmother during the period when their hostility and anxiety are directed against their mothers!

SOCIAL AND INDIVIDUAL FORCES

In our psychological approach, we differentiate between internal and external reality, and in speaking of maturation as the central task of adolescence, we are aware that the form, as well as the success or failure, of adaptation to external reality depends greatly on processes that take place in the internal world. While the sociologists refer to the role of general sociocultural forces in the adolescent's problems, we emphasize first the dependence of the effectiveness of these forces on psychological influences, and second the fact that the attitudes of the adolescents, as a social group in itself, are to a great extent determined by individual psychological processes. Later, we shall see how very much these processes influence and determine the formation of adolescent groups, regardless of their positive social values or their antisocial aims.

The striking variety of adolescent behavior depends largely on their unconscious fantasy life, on previous attachments, and on the degree of progress that they have made during childhood, in preparation for the last act of the growing process—i.e., for maturation into adolescence. In other words: maturation as a process takes place from the beginning of life; adolescence is only its last—very prolonged and very complicated—act; it is, at least theoretically, the resolution of the process. Many inner arrangements, rearrangements, and compromises have to be made in order to complete and even to set in motion this process of maturation. There is no doubt, on the other hand, that many psychological expressions of adolescence can be referred to directly as "sociological events," inasmuch as they are not only acted on the stage of social events, they are themselves a part of these events.

Future historians may be of the opinion that many of the happenings in which adolescence now plays an important role are in fact the results of various external factors: the general decrease of religious belief; preoccupation of the social environment with financial problems and local political events; devaluation of those who are supposed to be objects of successful identification; shocking contrasts in economic distribution; great emphasis on wealth and "success" on one side, and on the other the exclusion of many from participation in either, etc.

The developmental processes of adolescence make the adolescent especially prone to more or less rational (although always strong) reactions to the social situation, whether it be at home, or in society in its larger meaning. Some of these reactions are very typical and general: for example, devaluation of accepted values and the search for new ones; projection of one's own weaknesses and incapacities onto the outside; accusations, direct outbursts of aggressiveness, or overcompensation of inertia and passivity by acts of brutality. Great emphasis on values of social standing, and especially on intellectual performance; increased competition in fields that until now have been reserved for a small selected minority— these create in contemporary youth a tension of increased anxiety. Since these reactions are provoked by the social atmosphere, they are likely to lose their individual meaning in the broader perspective of the future looking back at the historical past.

The events that we witness, coupled with the evidence of "the teen-agers of our times in action," supply the sociologists with data for objective understanding and evaluation. The immediate approach of the psychologist, by contrast, may not be free from subjectivity, yet even his psychological interpretation of the forces that are expressed in social (or antisocial) acts is in our time likely to be rendered very much under the controlling influence of, or in collaboration with, the thinking of the general public. Reports of educational groups and of various social agencies, government participation, and above all the press, radio and TV serve to popularize, in one way or another, the insight gained and communicated by the psychologist. They are also, unfortunately, very often the source of a confusion that remains out of the psychologist's reach, even though he and his therapeutic efforts may be the chief victims of that confusion.

The battlefield of the adolescent's struggle is thus to be found on two fronts:

(a) the inner world of conflicts, which are to be resolved;

(b) the relationship to the external world (this refers both to their nearest and to their more remote environment), which needs to be stabilized.

In regard to the external world, we shall speak of adaptation and of the specific methods for achieving it in the developmental, transitional state of adolescence. Successful adaptation is one of the positive achievements of this process. External reality, in relation to an individual, is represented in part by himself—i.e., by *himself* as a part of this reality, and by his projections; above all, however, external reality means *other individuals*. This is what makes object relationships so extremely important: the adolescent's level of object relationship is a significant measure of his relationship to reality, and his full acceptance of it.

The basic goal of my work in this context has been to obtain an insight into the social activities of adolescents—more specifically, to investigate how the psychic forces that are typical of the period of maturation express themselves in the adolescent's relationship to social forces and institutions.

I have limited these investigations to group formations. Since groups are, after all, essentially aggregates of individuals, it was necessary to learn more about the trends that prevail among the individual adolescents of our time.

What I am reporting here is the results gained only in part by way of direct analysis. To a greater extent, they represent a macroscopic approach on the part of an analyst who has, for the time being, put aside the microscope of her profession. I have used all the opportunities possible: innumerable consultations of the sort described above; meeting young people socially; speaking with them, reading everything available to me that has been produced for them, better still by them —their letters as they have appeared in print, their published and unpublished literary productions, etc.

This approach was supported by the insight I have acquired through my own analytic experiences, as well as by the outstanding work on adolescents that has been done by other analysts. If I do not seem to be making more direct reference to the ideas of others in this paper, that does not mean that I am not aware of their influence on me and that I do not have the highest regard for the value of their work.

In our examination of the adolescent's relationship to the external world, we shall recognize to how great an extent that relationship is dependent on the internal situation—that is, on the solution of old and new inner conflicts—and to what degree the influence of external factors provides, in adolescence, what could be referred to as a new aspect to an old psychic situation.

An important role in our observations will be played by the process of adaptation, by struggles in the development of the ego, and by the impact of biological demands.

As we shall see, in this period each individual is going through a kind of personal revolution "in the service of the 'I.'" At the same time—in this generation, perhaps more than ever before—a strong attempt is being made to transform this personal revolution into a more general one, to

exchange the "I" for a "we." Our observations will lead us to
the recognition that in adolescence, as in many social upheavals, even when progress has been more or less achieved,
nothing altogether new is inaugurated, nor does anything old
come to a real and complete end. The process itself, as in all
revolutions, has as its goal to abandon old positions in favor
of new ones. We shall attempt to ascertain *what* these "new"
positions are and whether the process of maturation is really
a "revolution."

All phases of individual development—the whole history
of childhood *before* adolescence—represent an evolutionary
process, in which comparatively mild revolutions mark both
an end and a beginning. Yet the residue of each developmental phase is included in the next succeeding one, and
simultaneously progressive elements foreshadow their later
appearance, during the preceding developmental period.

Psychological events of later years—during adolescence—
show the same tendency. Periods that are described as "crises"
earn this appellation in part by the intensity of the events
that take place within them and in part by the fact that observation of them can now be more direct and objective than it
could previously. The social environment and the broad
external background have been enlarged. The fact that, even
during the maturity of motherhood, regressive elements are
intensified (H. Deutsch, 1945) is due to the fact that they had
been only submerged, and had never really been eliminated.

An influx of biologically predetermined sexual forces; the
inner perception of alterations that occur in the ego; new
reality demands and difficulties in adaptation—these are the
basic elements in the changes that take place during adolescence.

The ego now feels the impact of instinctual dangers. At the
same time, the superego assumes the role of a counterpower,
marshaling its forces against the instinctual invasion. The
kaleidoscopically fluctuating changes on the inner battlefield; victories of the instincts over the superego or vice versa;

the rejection or revival of previous identifications; the up-setting of the ego ideal; the search for new identifications; narcissistic engrossment and masochistic self-depreciation—all these are examples of the turmoil that occurs during the process of maturation.

The resulting tension and anxiety provoke new defensive measures, and it is the manifestation both of inner upheaval and of new defenses that creates the image of "the adolescent," as Anna Freud described it in her classic book (1936).

SUBLIMATION

During this period of inner turmoil, and in the midst of the struggle between the contrasting forces of action and agony, upheavals and overthrows, chaos and clarification, joy and despair—during all this, the development of the ego proceeds. Among the most important contributions to this development is sublimation. Some adolescents increase their capacity for sublimation and, in the midst of the inner fights, develop new skills and creativities. We can observe a poetic talent in search of the means of expression for a newly intensified fantasy life, for grief about vanishing childhood, for an only recently developed longing for new emotional contents, etc.

Unfortunately, the advent of maturity and the later adjustment to reality often combine to annihilate the adolescent's gains. In some few adolescents—this is often the case with unusually gifted children—the developmental struggles end with a marked impoverishment of previous capacities.

Whether or not the previous endowment does succumb to the negative forces of the adolescent process depends on the general outcome of that process. It is evident that, when the initial material that is present and at the disposal of sublimation is already well established, it can generally be imperiled only by strong neurotic elements. As we know, however, the counterforces of regression are increased during adolescence and may bring about a neurosis and with it an incapacity for sublimation. Many adolescent dropouts are victims of just such an inhibition of sublimation: I have known instances of suicide in which it was the unexpected difficulty with sublimation that created an unbearable narcissistic injury.

The interesting question arises whether the invasion of genital sexual energy does not also provide occasions for increased sublimation during adolescence. The assumption generally is that the sublimatory process depends on the pregenital forces and that the genital libido serves only direct sexual goals. Eissler (1963), in reference to Goethe's sexuality, makes an exception to the general rule, by asserting that "the genius may possibly acquire his unique capacities by the diversion of genital libido towards creation." Discussing this idea further, he expresses doubts "that a psychobiological organism can ever give up striving for the greatest possible pleasure with which nature has endowed the . . . organism" (p. 1404). This question is of great importance in regard to adolescence.

Years ago, Freud, in a meeting that was limited to a small number of participants, expressed his opposition to Wilhelm Reich's insistence that sexual activity should begin in adolescence—that is, as soon as the biological readiness is manifested. Freud regarded the *postponement of gratification* as an important element in the process of sublimation and thereby essential to development.

My own opinion is that, specifically in adolescence, the sublimation of genital sexuality plays an extremely important role and may often be the decisive element in the whole development.[4] The positive striving for genital gratification is still accompanied in adolescence by negative elements: ambivalence of emotions; guilt connected with masturbation; the incestuous character of fantasies; the narcissistic quality of love, even when related to objects; the tendency to identify with the objects, etc. One can observe that, despite successful genital activity, the sexual life of adolescents, even during

[4] I shall return later to this question, when I speak about earlier adolescent sexual activities.

their later period, does not psychologically reach the level of expected genital gratification. The reactive disappointment— the *omne animale post coitum triste est*—appears in adolescence more often than it does in later years, the urge for genital gratification being at this time due chiefly to a narcissistic emphasis on masculinity rather than to the strength of genital needs.

It has been my observation that an adolescent who invests his entire libido in genital gratification, for an overlong and energy-consuming period, suffers with regard to his capacity for sublimation, which may not fully recover during the process of maturation. Those intensive but unstable infatuations that are characteristic of adolescence have their specific role, to be sure: what they have to achieve is the resolution of incestuous attachments and of homosexuality. Yet they make their appearance at a time of transition, in which nothing is yet a real resolution, and when sexual activity may even bring a pathological reinforcement of old attachments. And, as mentioned above, permanency and intensity of sexual activity may bring disturbance in sublimation, especially during the earlier part of adolescence.

One might assume that pregenital regressions would produce material for sublimation. My own observations, however, of adolescents among whom the remnants of earlier developments are still in evidence seem to indicate that those remnants are likely to serve more primitive direct gratifications, rather than sublimations. Upon being deflected from the primary goal, they may appear as neurotic symptoms, or as deformities of personality, thereby confirming our assumption that it is the genital libido that constitutes the main source of sublimation in adolescence.

Let us not lose sight of the changes of external environment for the adolescent. The opening of new possibilities provides at the same time new outlets for sublimated energies, and thereby serves to direct the instinctual tendencies into ego functions. I think that my views on the postponement of genital gratification, even after biological maturation has been achieved, concur with the process of neutralization in action during adolescence (Hartmann, 1964).

One of the earliest achievements of sublimation "in the service of the ego" is the development of tenderness in early object relationships, a function that becomes of the greatest importance in adolescence. The opportunities provided to the social life of contemporary college students by coeducation seem very often to bring paradoxical results, with regard to the development of love as an emotional and sexual experience. My observations indicate that the looked-for harmonization of tenderness and sexuality runs into difficulties that are quite similar to those that were experienced by previous generations. Previously, the late adolescent made a direct and realistic division between "good (respected, admired) girl" and "bad (sexually approachable) girl." In our time, the young male makes this differentiation less consciously, and even protests upon being confronted with it.

The unconscious devaluation of a formerly highly regarded girl, following sexual intimacy with her, is often accompanied by grief, guilt feelings and, above all, astonishment on the part of the boy. These reactions provided, in quite a number of cases, the motive for the boy's seeking consultation: "I had such a wonderful friendship with her before." Apparently the image of the "chaste mother" is revived in this relationship, and the division between "sex" and "love" still persists. This does not, of course, completely exclude more mature and more harmonious relationships, which sometimes even lead to successful marriage. But it helps one to understand why events in college dormitories are not necessarily rendered less complicated by the relaxation of rules and the wisdom of tolerance. Evidently it takes more than one generation to overcome the personal and sociological past.[5]

[5] The attitudes of girls who find themselves involved in this situation will be discussed in Chapter 4.

INCREASE OF NARCISSISM

One may suppose that the ego enters the process of maturation in adolescence endowed with capacities that were developed previously. The problem now becomes the conservation of these capacities, their protection against the invasion of new instinctual forces, and their successful utilization for further developments.

One of the central problems of adolescence is the increase of narcissism and its vicissitudes. The later fate of this narcissism is a very important factor in the reaching of maturity.[6] What are the reasons for this increase of narcissism? Generally speaking, it is the result of the regressive trend that takes place in adolescence, not only in regard to instinctual drives but also in the ego.

We are here again confronted with the fascinating phenomenon of developmental progress as perhaps an *agent provocateur* for regression, in all the functions of personality. Such regressive phenomena can also be observed, as mentioned before, in pregnancy; there is also a full-scale analogy between adolescence and the climacterium, with regard to regressions, defense mechanisms, and attitudes, which are "too early" in adolescence and "too late" in the climacterium. There is even evident a tendency to repeat during the climacterium neurotic and psychotic states of adolescence.[7]

The developmental process of adolescence is accompanied by the loss of old objects before new ones have entered the emotional sphere. Gratifications that were earlier granted to the dependent and helpless child, in accordance with the pleasure principle, now give rise to reactions of disappointment and frustration in the maturing youth. The question

6 In a paper published in 1924 R. Waelder discusses a schizoid patient who was evidently kept from psychosis by his outstanding scientific interests and talent. His narcissism made him independent of other people and his immense capacity for sublimation kept him within the limits of sanity.

7 See H. Deutsch (1945, pp. 469-473). Grete Bibring (1959) considers pregnancy to be a period of "crisis" analogous to adolescence.

"Who will love me now?" is answered with "I, myself"—
another incentive to the increase of narcissism.

Another reason for the increase of narcissism is to be seen
in one of the most traumatic events of adolescence: the shat-
tering of the ego ideal, which is injured critically by the impact of sexuality, masturbatory guilt, increased severity of the
superego directed against the ego, and the latter's masochistic
reaction. The need to restore the image of one's own personality reinforces narcissism as a counterforce against self-
devalutaion and against the masochistic reactions to the
superego.

Another trauma—often one with disastrous consequences
—is the devaluation of the parental image (especially that of
the father). This is not generally the result of any increase of
cognitive capacity on the part of the maturing boy, although
he often couches it in terms that would seem to imply that
it is. The devaluation of the father as one member of the
sociological environment that is being criticized and rejected
by the adolescent serves merely as the rationalization of a
deeper process. It is one consequence of the regressive revival
of previous grandiose narcissistic fantasies, which were connected with the idealization of the paternal image. With the
revival of these fantasies, previous disappointments are also
reawakened; devaluation of the idealized object of earlier
identification may have a quite traumatic effect on the ego,
by contribuing to the increase of narcissism in adolescence.
Devaluation of the father thus serves to interfere with the
formation of the adolescent's own identity.

Our clinical experience makes us aware of the various consequences of the increase of narcissism in adolescence. One
example is the involvement of homosexual libido, in which
the narcissistic element may be the chief responsible factor.
Passionate ideal love, addressed by an adolescent to a younger
boy who is the image of one's own now weakened ego ideal,
is a very typical narcissistic object choice. My own observation seems to indicate that this form of adolescent homo-

sexuality is actually less ominous with regard to the possible later development of heterosexuality than an object choice that is built on the old relationship to the father, or on flight from the danger of incestuous love toward the mother. This form of adolescent homosexuality leads from the "ideal boy" to an "ideal girl," who is still endowed with the qualities of the boy's own ego ideal, yet constitutes a step forward on the way to real object relationship.

Nikos Kazantzakis, in his recently translated *Report to Greco,* gives a beautiful description of passionate homosexual love during the period of awakening interest for women: "as my flesh had awakened but it still did not know what features to give its desire—associating with a boy rather than a girl must have seemed much less dangerous to me, much more convenient—without wanting to or being aware of it, this homely, coarsely fashioned classmate had become a mask to hide women from me for a number of years." Here anxiety with regard to women employed homosexuality as a defensive action.

A very instructive example of the elementary forces that lead the adolescent to devaluation of the paternal image is afforded by insight into the psychological experiences of those youths who have been educated—rather, indoctrinated—to religious beliefs in strict Catholic schools. When one sees these boys, especially during early adolescence, turning to God and his representatives, one sometimes feels inclined to regret that this point of support—or something like it—is not available for the majority of contemporary youth.

Yet this only highlights the fact that religious belief itself falls under the impact of adolescent storms, so that often the struggle with the father is merely diverted to his most impersonal representative—God. The demons and devils that appear in the nightmares of these growing boys are soon identified as forces originating from within; the urge toward masturbation creates feelings of being "possessed." They therefore turn to God for help—only to find "Him" too to be ineffectual, weak, powerless.

I see such boys as these from time to time, on the recommendation of priest-teachers who are acquainted with psychoanalysis. After two or three interviews, we do not speak any longer about God and religious doubts; we speak about the real father, and the usual adolescent challenge to the godlike status with which the boy had endowed him during his earlier childhood. I have had some good results in these cases, when the therapeutic approach was directed toward the restoration of the Almighty, as represented by the "fathers" of the boy's school. We are always satisfied when the less pious adolescents achieve a good transference to their father substitute.

I have spoken at such length about the process of devaluation of the father in adolescence because I am convinced that among the most important tasks in the process of maturation are: to appease the superego and restore the afflicted ego ideal, and to reinforce the process of sublimation by identification with a rehabilitated father image. This identification must now be built on a phase-adequate cognitive experience, which replaces the old fantasy, in which the father was a representative of perfection in a narcissistic "I—you." A degree of overvaluation, as the expression of a positive relationship, is at this time acceptable and even welcome.

The fate of the deeply rooted identification with the father is the most important factor in the so-called "identity crisis" (Erikson) of adolescence. The adolescent's attitude toward the father will depend very much, of course, on developments in childhood—specifically, how much of the idealized image of the father was incorporated into the child's ego ideal and how much of it was repressed, only to reappear in a later regression, which repeats anachronistically the destiny of childhood: idealization and its epilogue, devaluation.

Increased narcissism may be a very positive factor in adolescence, not only as a defensive force against masochistic self-destructive elements, but also because it is a source for the transformation of energies into creative work, which is very valuable and important in the process of maturation. The relationship of narcissism to object love in adolescence is probably also one of transformation. The love-suffering adolescent is usually not really loving at all. If my observations are correct, in our times the adolescent is not very eager to indulge in any such Wertherian fate. Love for fun? yes; suffering? no!

As a matter of fact, the adolescent's narcissism is a reliable guardian of his emotional involvements, and the use of narcissistic cathexis is—as is evident from my observations, presented later in this study—the source of that aggrandizement of the ego that is very much needed in this period of the adolescent's life, yet at the same time is also quite ominous. Only when the pleasure principle has been replaced to a great extent by the reality principle is the adolescent ready for object love. This is a sign of ego strength and of progress in maturation, even though the struggle between narcissism and object love is still going on.

Heinz Kohut (1966) has discussed the part played by narcissism in the process of creativity and in empathy. His ideas are very validly applied to adolescence. Every gifted adolescent goes through a creative period (see Bernfeld's work [1924] on poetry-writing in adolescence). Unfortunately, this is sometimes the result of an inner process, which leads to a split between fantasy life and reality testing that often proves dangerous later on.

EMPATHY

With regard to empathy, it is quite typical of this period and quite widespread; indeed, one is tempted to regret that, with maturation, this positive component of the adolescent's ego is doomed to change. I shall not discuss here the genetic sources of this endowment. In adolescence, there is a close connection between empathy and the process of identification that is so typically reinforced during this period. It is also the

expression of an increased anxiety and tension, of a watchful-
ness that may lead to paranoid attitudes—that is, to the negative aspect of the same process that also contributes to the
development of the positive quality of empathy.

I think that another psychological process, which is very
similar to, if not identical with, empathy and is also characteristic of adolescence, is a kind of internal perception, a
special intuition concerning one's own internal processes
(H. Deutsch, 1939, p. 259). This increased capacity for intro-
spection is well known as a kind of clairvoyance in adolescent
schizophrenics, but it is also a part of normal adolescent functioning. While it has its positive values as a defense mechanism, it is, in addition, a very valuable servant of the precious
ability to "know yourself."

My impression is that the adolescents of our times are somewhat fearful of its use as a form of cognition, and prefer more
direct modes of the perception of reality. The more sophisticated among them may refer to Freud's conception of intuition, as expressed in *Beyond the Pleasure Principle:* "From
what I have seen of intuition, it seems to me to be the product
of a kind of intellectual impartiality" (1920, p. 59), and in
New Introductory Lectures: "there are no sources of knowledge of the universe other than the intellectual working-over
of carefully scrutinized observations . . . no knowledge derived
from revelation, intuition or divination" (1933, p. 159).

My own opinion is that empathy (like intuition) is the outcome of more complicated functions, in which "intellectual
impartiality" is a secondary elaboration of a deeper experience. Intellectual interpretation merely provides the rationality for irrational inner events.

Freud's attitude, quoted above, seems to be in contradiction to the fact that, in his writings, he often emphasized
the existence of the communication of unconscious mental
processes between two persons, as the result especially of emotional bonds between them. Freud's great adherence to intellectual "working over" did not interfere with his eagerness

to observe occurrences that are not easily understood in terms of pure rationality. He was even open to the interpretation of phenomena of a telepathic nature.

It is interesting to note that adolescents and women have in common this endowment of empathy (H. Deutsch, 1945). In the case of adolescents, as I indicated above, it is a defensive attitude that makes them deny their own sensitivity and emphasize instead the intellect.

REACTIONS TO SEXUAL MATURITY

I have referred again and again to adolescence as a battlefield of various forces. One event, biological in nature, constitutes the inauguration of sexual maturity and of those psychological events that Erikson (1956) calls the "adolescent crisis." During this period, the ego of the adolescent personality is in great need of support, yet paradoxically it has to provide this support out of its own resources. Against newly intensified impulses, it has to maintain the old defenses and create new ones; it has to consolidate achievements that have already been reached. The most important of its tasks is the struggle to synthesize all childhood identifications, as they become enlarged and enriched by new ones. The successful end result of this struggle will be the formation of a solidified personality, endowed with a subjective feeling of identity that is confirmed and accepted as such by society.

The regressive trend, as we have seen, brings with it a reawakening of the idealized parental image, which at this time undergoes devaluation, as well as difficulties with the ego ideal, which has to be restored. The difficulty in finding new objects with which to identify may be due, to some degree, to the character of our "affluent society," which evidently has not provided the younger generation with ideals and leaders.

Only simple, realistically inclined adolescents find in ready-made forms of living a refuge, in which a kind of identity is reached, without painful struggles and without deeper emotional involvements. The most comfortable place in this respect is father's business, with passive acceptance of his values but often also with the awakening of competitive conflict with father for authority.

During the ongoing struggle for identity, many more or less severe symptoms may arise. Inner perception of a lack of identity may be expressed by feelings of depersonalization or sensations of unreality; or it may appear in those "as if" personalities that are so often encountered in adolescence. During this period of life, "as if" phenomena can be regarded as a rather normal search for identity, which attaches this need to any object that is regarded as suitable, for a shorter or longer period. The general confusion of identity and the feeling of lacking coherence in his ego culminates in the adolescent's painful question, "Who am I?" Side by side with the struggle for identity, there may arise external difficulties in the process of socialization.

The adolescent lives his life, after all, between two worlds: one that has thus far complied with his demands and one that now demands his compliance. In loosening his ties to objects of the past, the adolescent is also giving up his previous social environment and its comforts. Infantile fantasies perpetuate the existence of this disappearing world; they give way only gradually to a more realistic conception of the new social actuality. The final realization and adjustment takes place simultaneously with the consolidation of identity, to form a harmonious unity. The last ego function of adolescence is the integration of the psychosexual and the ego aspects of the adolescent's life—an integration that can be successful only if the process of identification has ended with the establishment of harmony.

Another central problem of adolescence is the struggle between external, *objective* reality and inner, *subjective* reality. While the maturational process comprises both adaptation and an increased capacity for reality testing, nevertheless tension, anxiety, emotional deprivation, and the intensification of narcissism dissolve the borders of such a division: imaginary experiences may substitute for frustrating reality, and the outcome of the conflict between subjective and objective reality may be a more or less grave pathology.

The analyst has the best opportunity to observe such pathological distortions of the normal conflicts of adolescence. A patient whom I have treated analytically during all the years of his difficult adolescence provides a good example of the struggle between reality and fantasy life, in which we can recognize a pathological distortion of the normal conflict of adolescence. He will be dealt with in detail later.

The purely physiological act of sexual maturation may in itself become an event that provokes severe anxiety. Even though it is biologically determined, its impact upon the psychological reactions of the young person is immense and paradoxical. I shall not engage here in a discussion about the relationship between biological events and psychological phenomena.

In the analytic work, one is often surprised by the individual reactions of patients to events of a general nature. These reactions are viewed to begin with in the light of the patient's personal experience. Only when psychoanalytic observations confirm the insight that has been gained in individual cases do these observations become a part of knowledge.

The first ejaculation may constitute a *trauma* for the young man. The traumatic aspect is due, in the first place, to the fact that the event takes the young boy by surprise. He knew it would happen, and may even have looked forward to his "manhood" with impatience. Yet, according to my observation, the fact that active participation on his part is not involved creates in many boys a deeply traumatic reaction. In many cases, dreams and even masturbatory fantasies, upon being connected with ejaculation, become more destructive and dangerous.

The young man who has now come into the position of

being among the creators of new life feels himself to be dependent, for the fulfillment of this role, on an excrement of his body, which he tries to hide out of shame. The inability to control by his own will power the newly available physiological function creates in the recently matured individual the feeling that he is no longer the master of his body functions, that he is instead compelled to surrender to forces that are stronger than he is. In his attempts to free himself from the dependencies of his childhood, he easily falls victim to a new dependency, this time clearly derived from his own biology. At the very time when he is fighting to become the master of his impulses and infantile needs, he has instead become a slave. This deprivation of control, this feeling of surrender to inevitabilities, may constitute a trauma and lead to strong and sometimes permanent reactions.

While the largest number of adolescent boys confirmed these observations, a majority of adult men whom I interviewed denied it. The reason for this discrepancy is not altogether clear. Patients who have suffered enuresis in their childhood tend to compare these two events; both, they recognize, are independent of the patient's efforts and will. The general feeling can be formulated as follows: the ejaculation is experienced as a memorandum to the young man that he is not the master even of the physiological part of the house of his own body!

Two of my patients who first enlightened me about the physiological trauma of adolescence were not adolescents but middle-aged men. They were quite different in their personalities and in the nature of their neuroses, yet their experiences in adolescence had been very similar. They had both reacted with profound disturbance to their first ejaculation, and they were both able even then to achieve control over the repetition of that event by their own efforts. Patient A. was able to stop his erections before he felt the approach of the peak of his sexual excitement; patient B. had a feeling of real victory: he enjoyed to the full his fantasies and his erections, and yet reached such a degree of mastery that he was able at will to end an erection without an ejaculation.

After a time, I came to recognize that the peculiarities of my two patients, who were unique in regard to their active intervention in the physiological act, were in both instances a distortion and at the same time an intensification of that inner protest that is so often encountered in adolescence. It may not be too farfetched to suggest that the "surrender" the adolescent is called on to make is actually adding to, reinforcing, and perhaps in some individuals even giving rise to the protest against the "mastery" of his environment over him.

Anna Freud (1958) speaks about cases of impotence who, during their analyses, recovered memories of practices that they had carried out in adolescence, which had at that time served them either to prevent erections or to suppress them as soon as they occurred. I assume that, in these patients, as in those I myself observed, masturbation conflicts and castration anxiety account for the peculiarities of their practices. The significant experience of my patients—the immediate goal that they not only intended but reached—was the triumph of will over the bodily functions. These patients did not suffer impotence in their mature life; instead, their ego was endowed with a kind of stubborn energy that was at their disposal in other situations that also called for "mastery," even though these latter situations had nothing directly to do with the conquest of a biological trauma.

THE POSTADOLESCENT PHASE

It is generally agreed that adolescence comes to an end after a painful struggle, of greater or lesser duration, and makes way for the state of maturity.

The beginning of the so-called "adolescent crisis" is not as clearly defined as its end; yet, even when the theoretical conditions are fulfilled, the resolution is always only partial. Blos (1962) correctly emphasizes that the conflicts are only in part resolved at the close of adolescence, and that ego synthesis therefore is required to incorporate the not yet resolved remnants of early childhood.

Even when the ego has achieved the victory of the reality principle over the pleasure principle, and the ego ideal and superego have attained the consolidation of their goals; even if diffused sexuality has reached the level of genital organization and the process of adaptation has fulfilled its role—still, the strenuous process of adolescence is never, perhaps, definitely concluded. The unresolved residua may appear in later life, in spite of the fact that the adolescent himself, as well as the persons of his social environment who are involved in the struggle—directly or indirectly, and often very painfully —look forward to the blessings of "maturity" in the immediate future.

The period that follows adolescence is so laden with the residua of these struggles that one is inclined to assign to it a separate place in developmental history. We may be disappointed in our expectations, however. An analogy with the therapeutic process of analysis comes to mind. I am aware that there is no assurance, even after a successful analysis, that the patient's neurotic difficulties will not be revived by later events. The upheaval of adolescence may be compared with the efforts of analysis, in that there is no certainty that the conquered forces of childhood will not be, under certain conditions, later reactivated.

Observations of the period that follows even a successful termination of adolescence nevertheless permit the conclusion that this period has certain definite aspects of its own, and I would suggest the marking off of a "postadolescent" phase. It is true—just as it was in adolescence itself—that individual differences will later come into action, thus giving this phase a certain variety. I exclude from these observations those young people who during their adolescence suffered irreversible traumata, were involved in reality situations that were difficult to solve, or showed gross pathology. The real-life situation will itself contribute either positive or negative forces to the postadolescent's further maturation. A high degree of sexual maturity, postambivalent relationship to people, and the consolidation of the ego ideal and of the superego are usually still expected to be stabilized at the end of adolescence. My observations seem to prove that in actuality this is never, or at least very seldom, the case. I have specifically in mind here a type of patient whom I quite often had the occasion to observe. They undertook their analyses, not because they suffered a neurotic illness; instead, they themselves, even though they were considered to be "normal," felt a need for "improvement."

My own diagnosis, my chief reason for accepting them as patients, was the anxiety that lay hidden behind their relatively well-functioning defenses. They were usually young men who were successful in their social and professional activities. Their sexuality was satisfactory, their marriage was stabilized, and often they were fathers. Their analysis was usually burdened from the beginning with intellectual knowledge. They were very eager to bring infantile material and looked very eagerly for "mother transference," assuming that this was what was expected of them, etc. When one obtained more insight into all aspects of their "normal personality," however, one discovered that, under a mask of maturity, under the cover of a good adjustment, the unsettled forces of adolescence still continued to be present. These appeared in an acting out of adolescent fantasies, and in a kind of activity that had been uncontrolled and irrational in the past, but was now more restricted and more adjusted to a relative normalcy. Their actual character, as a continuation of adolescence, was in effect disguised.

In analysis, it takes time before the analyst discovers that the normal sexuality of the patient is involved in an abundance of sexual foreplays, which have been accepted as pleasurable additions, but are in fact expressions of the need for infantile gratifications that were mobilized during adolescence. Such a patient's preoccupation, for example, with his wife's lack of orgasm (which he expects to be similar to his) is based on his need for constant confirmation of his masculinity, which evidently still suffers from adolescent uncertainty. His ego ideal and superego are still bound to identifications; if one observes his relationships to friends and to superiors, one sees the adolescent as no longer in turmoil but involved in a relatively controlled acting out. In the analytic situation, this acting out is reinforced, yet its manifestations are often overlooked.

Experience with these patients has confirmed for me the observation by A. Freud (1958) and by Lampl-de Groot (1960) that adult patients do not speak about their adolescence. My work with adolescents has made me see more clearly than I did in the past that their developmental problems actually extend more or less fully into the age of "maturity." It is the events in the postadolescent period—the acting out—that seem to be responsible for the fact that they do not speak about their adolescence: since they are still involved in it, they can at this time only "act it out"—which may also be true of many of our "mature" patients.

Anna Freud (1958) has remarked that the memory of an experience in adolescence is in fact divided: the events are easily remembered, but emotional reactions are in amnesia. Yet in her description of adolescence, she herself explains this peculiar phenomenon. While these emotions may be very powerful, they lack consistency: they fluctuate; they change and easily subside. I think that their chances of being remembered are weak from the beginning. If the individuals have suffered great traumata in adolescence, these evidently had no direct impact upon them. The adolescent is so preoccupied with his painful inner struggles that his attitude toward traumata that occur in reality is quite infantile. Specifically, his grieving after an actual loss is like that of a child: the adolescent's ego is still too weak to cope with the mourning, and the emotional reactions are absorbed during the process of adolescence and often delayed. On such occasions, we hear complaints by members of their social environment: "He (or she) is so *heartless.*"

(With regard to psychoanalytic candidates-in-training, it should be noted, the organization of the Institutes creates a ready-made psychological atmosphere for the kind of acting out described above. The wild competition with colleagues: "who will graduate sooner?"; the peer identification in terms of their relationship to teachers; the eagerness to exalt one's own analyst to the position of ego ideal and superego—all this is ready-made for intensification of the acting out that is characteristic of the postadolescent period.)

This acting out, incidentally, may be the reason why the analysand is eager to bring the expected (as he thinks) infantile material (Lampl-de Groot, 1960), rather than those events of his adolescence in which he is still involved. Intensification of such acting out may sometimes create difficulties, however: the analysand's colleagues complain about the aggressiveness of his competition, while his professional superiors observe in him an unreasonable rebelliousness, etc. Acting out in this period is a kind of finishing process, but it may also have the defensive role of preventing the after-repression of the not-quite-buried forces of adolescence. (I do not think that "finishing" here means really "the end.")

There are men who remain in adolescence until old age; their climacterium is actually not a revival but rather a reinforcement of their long-standing continuation of their adolescence.[8]

---

[8] An impressive eternal adolescent is Martin Luther, as he is brought to life in Erikson's biographical drama (1958).

CHAPTER 2

SOME FORMS OF OBJECT RELATIONS IN ADOLESCENT BOYS

The chief aim of this study is to deal with the psychological forces that motivate the group formations of adolescents, which are so impressive in their variety, yet—as observation seems to show—stem from the same dynamic forces as more commonly known activities of a directly individual character.

This makes it advisable for us to turn our attention to those individual expressions, typical as they are of adolescence, before discussing the psychological forces that are operative in group formations. For this purpose, I shall use clinical experiences that I have gained during the course of the psychoanalytic treatment of adolescent patients.

One case that I have analyzed provides me with the opportunity to discuss at this point two basic problems of adolescence:

(1) the conflict between reality and fantasy—that is, between external and internal reality—and the ways in which the adolescent tries to solve that conflict; and

(2) the balance between narcissism and object relationship, and how it is maintained.

GIFTED ADOLESCENTS: CASE REPORTS

The patient I speak of first came to analysis as a seventeen-year-old boy. He had a variety of symptoms; to him, however,

42

the most painful fact was that, while his "only goal in life" was to become a writer or a poet, he was unable to write creatively.

George had been an extraordinary child: when he was only three and a half years old, he was already able to read and write; at the age of five, he wrote poetry and stories that, without any doubt, revealed the presence of an unusual talent. He himself had fantasies of being a genius. From his early childhood ("from the beginning of my life," as he put it), he was a lonely child: he liked to be left alone with his books, his daydreams, and his writing, and withdrew more and more into isolation. When he was six or seven years old, he began to show his first neurotic symptoms. His parents thereupon consulted a well-known Swiss child psychiatrist, under whose care the boy remained until the family moved to the United States, a year before he started his analytic treatment.

The Swiss psychiatrist had done remarkable work; he had perhaps saved the boy from psychosis. The therapy had consisted primarily of active efforts to bring the boy out of his isolation and to keep him in continuous contact with reality. During that time, George attended boarding schools and camps and participated in a great many activities; his earlier creativity did not continue, however, and, with the help of his therapist, he gradually gave up making any efforts to realize his dreams of glory.

It seems amazing now that he did not deteriorate mentally, following this act of renunciation. In all the schools he attended, he succeeded in remaining a good, above-average pupil. Although he had "friends," his real object relationships—as was demonstrated in his analysis—were very weak and lacking in constancy on his part. Under the cover of his "activities," he remained actually rather passive; his aggressiveness came to the fore only from time to time, in outbursts of violent anger. Although his earlier symptoms persisted, a marked improvement became evident.

During his first year at college, George was very depressed and anxious; yet he continued to be a good mixer in the college's social life. In keeping with the mores of his particular group, he drank too much and surrendered from time to time passively to a homosexual relationship, without being emotionally aroused. At that time, he had not yet had any heterosexual experiences. His fight against masturbation was successful: he achieved complete abstinence, with a certain degree of pride and with the feeling of being a person with a strong will!

He remained a good student up to the point when recollection of the period in which he had been a "genius" was reawakened in his mind; it had always been there, but had been blocked off by his strenuous efforts in the direction of reality. He now tried various compensations for his heightened narcissistic demands: his social ambitions increased; in his desire to impress his classmates with his parents' social status, he spent money lavishly, and played the role of the *grand seigneur;* his clothes were extremely elegant, etc.

With all this, George became at the same time more and more depressed; the despair that resulted from his feeling that he was not, after all, a genius even brought him close to suicide. On the advice of his parents, he then entered analysis. It soon became evident that here was a "frustrated genius," who hoped to re-establish his lost identity by way of treatment. While the transference was established, the usual psychoanalytic technique could not be followed.

In the second (or third?) year of his analysis, his work in college, after a long period of slackening off, once again improved. His writing came to the attention of one of his teachers, and his fantasy of being a genius now began to acquire a grain of reality. He presented this teacher with a collection of his own poetry, pretending that the poetry had been written by an unknown French medieval writer, and that he was merely its translator. Since I was part of his secret world, he confided the truth about this to me. He rejected any expression of appreciation on my part, however, or any indication that I considered him to be talented (as I really did).

He continued to write, but always with the anxious feeling that being a genius as a writer might lead him to the disaster of isolation and insanity. His further development was quite satisfactory. Subsequently, after many years of a very good (but not brilliant) career, he expressed his gratitude to me. Nevertheless, he did not consider his analysis to have been successful, since the role of genius had not ever been restored to him during his treatment.

In considering this patient's case, we can come, I think, to the following conclusion: during his adolescence, the intensification of his narcissistic strivings had reawakened the old childhood dream of glory, that of being "the genius." The impact of this reawakening was too strong, however, the memory of the past too vivid, for him to accept mere fantasies as a realization of this dream of glory. He would have had to act upon—evidently he had preserved (under a block) —a certain amount of talent in order to achieve it.

The real reason for his denial of his identity as a genius poet, therefore, was his anxiety about losing contact with reality and becoming once again lonely and isolated, as he had been at the time when he was a gifted child. Just as he had rid himself of his dangerous genitals by an imaginary castration, so he had rid himself of his "genius" by denying his creative identity. Indeed, behind the medieval figure he had concocted to cover his creative ego lay his anxiety lest his writing prove to be an action taken against the reality principle, against his own normality. For that reason, his actual existence followed a vicious cycle: on the one hand, he had sacrificed his sexuality to his ardent wish to be a writer; yet, at the same time, he had to sacrifice his creative identity in order to conform with reality and to ensure the protection it offered him against his dreaded loneliness and isolation.

In such cases—when they occur under more favorable conditions—the childhood genius persists until the trials of adolescence set in. Sometimes the genius's downfall comes very early, and the process of deterioration takes a neurotic or even a psychotic form. Nothing—not even a recollection—survives that sort of catastrophe. At times, the deterioration is a slower process, and the end result is relative normality, burdened only by the unfulfilled promises of destiny.

Norbert Wiener was one of the survivors of the prodigy-genius syndrome. In his autobiography (1953), he describes the tragedy of complete disintegration and insanity that he himself had observed in a genius who had been a contemporary of his. There is also a very interesting case of a boy who, in early childhood, had been diagnosed by the experts as being a hopeless case of autistic psychosis. He did improve to some degree, yet he never succeeded in approaching psychic normality. An unusual talent persisted, in a certain branch of the sciences—a talent that was further developed during the period of his isolation and his very hazy contact with reality. In adolescence, his ability to sublimate was so strong that he was accepted by a college of the highest intellectual standards, and at a considerably younger age than usual; his talent, in short, was preserved in spite of the persistence of his mental abnormality, and the deterioration of his personality as a whole.

Direct observations of exceptionally gifted children have given me the impression that the psychological events in the life of the patient (George) I presented earlier may be regarded as being to a large degree typical, even though this insight was gained through treatment of one particular form of psychopathology.[1]

We often confuse precocity with genius.[2] Exceptional

[1] See also the report by Loomie et al. (1958), on the "Gifted Adolescent Project," started by Ernst Kris at the New York Psychoanalytic Institute.

[2] I think that George, for example, was precocious, but not by any means a genius.

children generally earn the title of "genius" primarily because of the unusual timing, rather than the character of their performances. Nevertheless there do exist especially gifted individuals who, during their childhood, have already shown evidence of unusual creative talents. Special attention should be given to differentiating between these two qualities.

The life history of an unusually gifted person can seldom be known completely and objectively, because immediate and direct observation is usually possible with regard to only one end of his development: either the childhood is observed and the future predicted from it; or else the mature period is known and the childhood is reconstructed on the basis of biographical (or autobiographical) data. As to biographical data, we know how relatively superficial and subjective these are; as far as autobiographies are concerned, Camus, is probably correct when he says that "Man often retraces the history of his nostalgias and temptations—almost never his own biography."

Since the mature life of a creative personality is somewhat easier to observe directly, it may be of value here to communicate certain direct observations (still somewhat rare) on especially gifted children who demonstrate the promise—but so far only the promise—of great achievement in the future. An accurate evaluation of the chances that this promise will be fulfilled can usually be given by the time of adolescence.

Before we discuss the adolescence of "geniuses," let us turn our attention to events of their childhood. An opportunity for the direct observation of three such individuals was given me by their parents; later, when they had reached their adolescence, these three were to come again into the focus of my attention.[3]

I was able to study very closely these three little children (two boys and one girl), who were marked with "genius." While the boys' talents were very similar, the girl's was dif-

[3] In all three cases, one of the parents had been, during his (and her) own earlier years, in analysis with me.

ferent. All three had shown from their earliest childhood an intensity of observation and of reactivity that indicated great intelligence. It soon became evident, however, that their real interest was not in the customary activities of children.

One had the impression that they were really themselves only when they were alone. As long as they lived in their own world, and nothing from the outside invaded their concentration, they were friendly, serene, and content—sometimes even ecstatically happy. When they were required to detach themselves from their absorption, they usually made themselves ready to readjust to a different task, but still of an intellectual character. If this was not available, however, they became depressed; even when they were participating in activities with others, they were clearly detached.

Depressive moods were frequent, especially when they were confronted with external reality. Their preoccupation with their inner world had created in time a loneliness of a special kind: it was a concentration on something that had no form and therefore could not be communicated. This is probably what Greenacre (1962) and Hitschmann (1956) have called the "pre-creative period." The creative urge, which had developed very early, now manifested itself as a search for means of expression. In two of these children—the boys —this search was at first unspecific; then it crystallized into a definite branch of science. For both boys, every bit of play, every way of being occupied was immediately turned into an arena for creativity, until it had become stabilized into a definite form, along the lines of their specific talent. The girl, on the other hand, was preoccupied from the start with visual matters; her talent for painting had become evident quite early.

In the subsequent development of these children (during latency), conflict with reality came as a disturbance to their peaceful isolation. This seems to be a general fate of young geniuses. At a certain age, the impact of reality becomes more and more powerful, so that the future of the gifted child

seems to depend on the harmonious interplay between creative loneliness and the call of reality (that is, narcissistic and
object cathexis). If it is the loneliness that prevails, then the
child may become an isolated exile in a hostile world and,
instead of creativity, pathology may develop. This was the
case, for example, with my patient George. Normally, the
conflict between inner and outer reality persists in varying
degrees. But as the tools for expression begin to become
available—for the painter, the brush; for the poet writer, the
pen; for the creative scientist, devotion to science and the
laboratory—object relationships begin to crystallize. These
are very much conditioned by creative interests: it is that
part of the world that can be characterized by the preoccupation as a help and not as an interference that is positively
cathected. Identifications, too, are to a large extent determined by the ability of the objects of identification to collaborate in the prosecution of the "great task."

My conclusion from these observations is that the conflict
between the powerful inner reality of the creative mind and
the impact of external reality was present from early childhood, in the geniuses with whom we are now dealing. In his
paper on "Creative Passion of the Artist and Its Synesthetic
Aspects" (delivered in commemoration of Ernst Kris), Felix
Deutsch (1959) expressed the idea that "The creative product
is the triumph of unity" and spoke of the "materialization of
the object lost in struggle and now revived." Phyllis Greenacre (1957) has very impressively described the "double life"
of the artist, and especially the peculiarities of his external
personal life, which are so often in direct contrast to his
creativity. Both Felix Deutsch and Phyllis Greenacre had in
mind the problem of artists; my observations, however, have
to do with scientific creativity.

The ancient myths of Prometheus, on the one hand, and
Epimetheus, on the other, express the duality of this conflict
between creativity and reality. A more modern version of

this same conflict has given us Don Quixote and Sancho Panza as the protagonists (see H. Deutsch, 1937a).

The problem of the relationship between genius and insanity is not germane to my theme. Unfortunately, however, adolescence sometimes confronts us with this problem.[4]

I have so far discussed the conflict between the genius's creativity and reality, or, more specifically, between the narcissistic ego and the object world. Up to adolescence, the process of adaptation in the three children I observed was not grossly impaired: these children were endowed with a marked capacity for a number of sublimated activities. Only the existence of specific talents that were at the core of their genius showed that we were confronted not merely with a capacity for sublimation, but also with a property of the ego that can be regarded as constitutional.

The capacity for object relationship was evidently fragile from the beginning, although adaptation to the routine aspects of living was excellent. The boys possessed many gifts and interests, but, sooner or later, most of these were sacrificed on the altar of their specific talent. All their other sublimations suffered a fate identical to that which characterized their relationships with people: they appeared and subsided and then reappeared—but only when strong provocations, or demands for their presence, came forward (school assignments, for example). With regard to both children, one had the impression that, as to the general impoverishment of their life as a whole, that sacrifice was made so that they might have available for focused employment their inner wealth, so passionately guarded by them in the encapsulated safe-box of the "genius."

It is hard to determine whether difficulties in object relationships, along with a more general weakness in regard to those values in life that are conditioned by external objects,

---

[4] Pissarro once wrote to a friend, after meeting young Van Gogh: "He will be either a great artist or insane." Some years later, he wrote to the same friend: "I did not know that he would be both."

are the result of insufficient neutralization (Hartmann, 1955). From my own observations, I would conclude that the primary reason for the existence of these problems is the continual concentration of all of the genius's ego abilities in one single direction. Whatever the reason is, these unusually gifted individuals fail in the process of integration, with the consequence that their talents and abilities, which were originally outstanding, succumb to a process of deterioration.

It is clear, I think, that forces involving the outside world —above all, object relationships—are experienced as dangerous threats to the security of the genius's narcissistic stronghold. It is only recognition of that fact that makes possible a better understanding of his loneliness, his longing for objects, his joy in finding these objects, and his subsequent horror at their loss and, finally, the sacrifice that must be made in this situation, either of the "genius" or of the objects.

In such a situation, equilibrium is seldom reached. What complicates the situation for the "genius" is the fact that his performance is on such a high level, so far above that of his contemporaries, that the stamp of "genius" is, in effect, *imposed on him from the outside*—with the result that the growing child's own internally motivated isolation is intensified by the actions and attitudes of those around him.

In adolescence, the whole inner situation is rendered more complex by the advent of the biological impact of sexuality —that is, intensification of the drives; revival of the oedipal situation; reactions by the superego; and, above all, the trauma to the ego ideal. Soon, all the inner forces that have till then been sublimated in the "genius" are given new life, in the struggle between object relationships and the "genius's" narcissistic position. From then on, the character of the final outcome of the struggle begins to take shape.

From this point on, I am limiting my observations to the two boys whom I knew from their childhood; I did not observe directly the further development of the girl painter. I know that she is still considered to be very talented and

promising but also that, during her adolescence, her erotic
life became quite stormy and intrusive. One of the boys re-
minds me to some degree of George, in that his handling of
his problem represents in a more concentrated form essentially George's way of dealing with it. Facing reality and his
loneliness, he gave up for a time, during adolescence, his
preoccupation with creative interests: he rejected further
education, and spent two years in various jobs, including
some manual labor, after which he finally returned, willing
to compromise, to his previous concerns. His talents were
now put to use in concrete experimental work; as a graduate
student, he is no longer the "genius," although he is a very
promising scientist. He is definitely, however, an obsessional
neurotic.

The second boy, during his adolescence, went through a
period of depression, marked by desperate feelings of loneliness. He, too, turned his back for a time on his previous devotion to science; later, however, he also returned to this
earlier interest. As far as I have been able to discover, this
boy's psychological makeup is typical; it is indeed often
found in scientists. His object libido is rather weak and
deficient in constancy, and his feeling of loneliness recurs
whenever his absorption with scientific problems is insuffi-
ciently strong. We do not find him associating with any particular groups; his contacts with people seem to be used for
the most part as a defense against loneliness, which he en-
dures in the name of his devotion to "pure science."

Another type of individualistically oriented adolescent is
the brilliant honors student. Let us call one typical student
of this kind Arnold. Boys like him were formerly encountered only in the top universities, but now they are found
with increasing frequency, and on more and more campuses,
as the result of the swelling of enrollments in colleges and
universities all over the country. These students are dedi-
cated to their classwork, to the exclusion of all other interests. They are the young scientists, devoted to the most

exact investigation of scientific material, not so much in the physical as in the historical and social sciences.

As scholars in these sciences, they are interested in specific events and other such data—in short, in all materials that make use of their ability to memorize. The human factors that are involved in these events, however, hold no interest for them. They usually have an excellent memory; they keep to written material and select as their future goal one that does not demand of them any form of affective partnership. They concentrate on learning, memorizing, gathering knowledge—all out of already known sources. They will perhaps accomplish a lot—short, however, of creativity. They do not want to be confronted with problems of the sort that call for profound human understanding or for struggle with contradictions in thinking; nor are they willing to suffer risks and uncertainties, or to become involved in abstractions. Their exact knowledge of facts, along with the precision and accuracy of their communications, makes them respected members of the scholastic community; yet their lack of imagination, or of constructive speculation, leaves their scientific approach rather sterile. As time goes by, they acquire the reputation of being brilliant bores.

These are often the highest honor students, for whom obtaining this external proof of recognition—being regarded in some particular respect as "the best"—is the central goal of their existence. Their adolescence remains uneventful. Very little struggle takes place in it: the maturation process is completely taken up with learning and with achieving the highest grades. The rest of their emotional development actually remains stalled at the level of their adolescence, and their future can be easily predicted. When they are not obliged, for financial reasons, to make an early start at earning their living and supporting a family, they become instead professors at an early age, and repeat—over and over again—the triumphs of their adolescence. They are "brilliant" but limited teachers, just as they were "brilliant" but limited students.

These individuals belong among the lonely young men. They have no real friends or lovers; they are grateful not to be disturbed in the achievement of their direct goals. The learning process itself is, for them, a source of pleasure; above all, it is a perfect refuge from external activities. They are, in all aspects of living, quite passive, and they embrace this "enforced" passivity very eagerly. They build no defenses against it; instead, they regard being "a real man" as a rather negative sort of achievement. Their passivity is in reality a grandiose protection against any interference with their chosen aim of absorbing vast quantities of knowledge and thus becoming recognized, in some corner or other of human endeavor, as the "best." They are, to a large degree, uncreative—but without feeling frustrated about it.

I had no opportunity to investigate analytically this type of adolescent boy. But as an analyst I have known such people in their mature and highly successful lives. During their formative years, they were absorbed in learning, and gratified by great successes; at that time their loneliness was welcome. Now, in their maturity, they may suffer from depression. Up till then, no special effort was necessary: they enjoyed the recognition of both young and old, and were able to look on success and respect as theirs. But now there is no longer any triumph in being the best, and they feel that all their work has been to no avail. One of my patients became depressed, for example, when he discovered that courses offered by his colleagues, who were less learned than he, were enjoying a far greater popularity among students than his own. He was no longer in the "highest honors" bracket!

In recent years, the numbers of this type of student seem to have grown. From my insight into the life of these adolescents, there emerge certain similarities of pattern. They belong among those intellectual boys whose development reflected from the start their intensive bond with the mother, concomitantly with the father's neglect of his paternal role. These are the mothers who, in the conflict between their own need for personal achievement and their motherhood, have found a definite solution; they are often able to continue their own earlier goals successfully (although sometimes they give these up in favor of their role as mothers). In such cases as these, the son—usually the only, or the oldest child in the family—is included in the mother's ambitions, in a kind of intellectual symbiosis. In this relationship, the narcissism is gratified on the part of both mother and son: they can go along in a highly sublimated love relationship, without suffering any feelings of guilt. The father is, of course, devalued and rejected—as a result of which these boys seem to escape stronger involvements in the oedipus complex.

During adolescence, a short masturbatory period creates some problems. Following the successful handling of these problems, there is a new wave of sublimation and the boy is able to present to the mother new progress in scholastic achievement. These boys seldom look for therapeutic help; my own insight was gained, not from them, but from the treatment of men whose adolescence had in this same sense been extremely "successful." Once an adolescent boy of this type did come for therapeutic help: he was suffering from depression and feelings of depersonalization, after he discovered that his mother was involved in an affair with a very "stupid man." I presented him with the possibility of treatment. Characteristically, he discussed this consultation with his mother, who then took over the situation. I never heard anything further from him.

Dealing with this sort of adolescence is very instructive: it reveals that, under certain conditions, a sublimated alliance with the mother, and the avoidance of stronger involvement in oedipal problems, can have a very positive effect on the boy's intellectual development. But it also shows the existence of a negative side, in impoverishment of emotional life and

in a lack of imagination and creativity. Deficiency in masculine identification is responsible to a high degree for passivity, and probably as well for weakness in sexual genital
strivings.

Arnold represents only one type of individual developed
as the result of narcissistic union with the mother. Some years
ago, I was able to observe a closely similar psychological situation, but under completely different social conditions. I am
speaking now of boys who are reared and educated in a
deeply religious atmosphere of strong Catholic beliefs. Here
the Catholic dogma of the Holy Virgin and the Christ-child
plays an immense role. From his birth, the boy's vision is
focused on possible sainthood; his immediate focus is the
profession of priest. The mother's ego ideal and the boy's
primary narcissism find their common expression in the
attempt to realize these religious goals (see H. Deutsch, 1964).

In my observations of contemporary "brilliant" youth, I
have found confirmation for the ideas expressed in this paper,
to the effect that such a union with mother can—under certain conditions—lead to a very successful development.

A great many of these "brilliant" students demonstrate,
from their earliest childhood, that they possess great intelligence and indubitable talents. These qualities may be called
into action by their mother's great expectations for them and
by her admiration. Since such students are often well adapted
to reality, they are able, later on, to produce real achievements. Their highest goals, during the years of their late
adolescence, are to attain Phi Beta Kappa and to become a
future "Nobel Prize winner" (Tartakoff, 1966).

Very often, however, it is responsible for a morbid ambition (as in Arnold's case) that is concentrated on successes.
This is expressed, to begin with, in the choice of a prestige
college and a possible traumatic reaction to not having been
accepted by it. Later, it becomes a crippling hunt for honors,
which interferes with the real development of often outstanding intellectual capacities.

Characteristic of all of them is the victory of narcissism over emotional ties to external objects. They often succeed in attaining high social positions, and generally their goals reflect the actual cultural values of their society. They are usually top honor students; but, according to my experience, even in adolescence they feel themselves threatened by competition, and by an emotional vacuum that they are not always able to tolerate. Since Arnold was never actually in this danger, his frustration came only in later years. From his early years, however, George was torn, as we have seen, between his narcissistic goals and his relationship to the object world, and it was only with psychiatric help that he was able to decide in favor of the latter. Yet he remained neurotically sick. I do not believe that Arnold would ever have considered deciding *against* his narcissism, as George did.

Our contemporary world is widely populated, I think, by "brilliant youths" with the same basic problems as those that were true of the young men described above. In a great many cases, their developmental history is similar: the involvement of what may be genetic factors in their narcissism; precociousness of intellectual endowment; reinforcement of their mother's own narcissism by the son's promising development; and in most of the cases, by far, the father's role as frustrating for the boy. All these are evidently decisive factors in the development of the boy's personality. I call this relationship with mother *folie à deux,* and regard it as a phenomenon that is in part closely linked to the cultural milieu in America, but is not restricted to the goals of certain social groups. "My son, the Nobel Prize winner," can easily be replaced by "My son, the college student," or "My son, the teacher"—depending on the social level.

This attitude also makes its appearance in a different sort of culture—for example, in socially rejected minority groups, for whom each step upward in the social scale is a great achievement, the realization of a fantasy. I take as one ex-

ample the typical Eastern European orthodox Jewish family.[5]
In these families, the mother is the head of the family, responsible for the mental and physical health of the children.
She has *de facto* authority in the family; the father is a more
remote figure—psychologically, and often literally. He may
be away from home a great deal: "children, household [and
often their support] are not man's business." This absence on
the father's part becomes part of the family picture: even
when he is at home, he is not an active participant in the
family circle, but is preoccupied with his own concerns. In
strictly orthodox circles, the father's preoccupation is with
God and with his pious friends. He spends his day praying
and studying the holy books, and leaves all the realities of
daily life to his wife. She is not only the custodian of the
family and the educator of her children; in many such families, she is also the breadwinner, the only real support of the
children.

This does not mean that the father is an unrespected, in-
ferior figure. Quite the contrary, his closeness to God (if this
is an orthodox family) makes him a respected, though remote
person. But it is with the mother, in the end, that the children share their future—their aspirations, ambitions, goals.
It is she—with *her* ambitions and efforts—who directs the
children's way to the future especially that of the oldest son,
who is the family "genius." *He* will some day reach the
heights, socially and financially. Since in this society there
are very few professions among which a Ghetto Jew can
choose, this son will be "a doctor." The son grows up in a
kind of secret union with his mother: *he* will be the reward
for her love and sacrifices.

This burning ambition, this narcissistic involvement—developed in terms of a childhood union with the mother—is
also an expression of filial indebtedness. I have seen men

[5] I have had the opportunity to observe this sociologically interesting group
directly. Excellent information on this is provided in *Life Is with People* by
Zborowski and Herzog (1952).

who, after being separated from their mothers early in their lives by political tragedy, have found in new countries successes that would never have been attainable in their own country. Yet some of these men display a neurotic restlessness and, over and over again, change their professions, their environments, etc. Others, by contrast, do achieve peace and harmony, an excellent professional and good family life. Yet from time to time it happens that a man with this background has reached, after long and difficult training, the coveted goal that he had first formed at the time of his difficult adjustment to his new country, and is now ready to take over the role of father of an American family. A time for relaxation seems to have arrived. Suddenly, however, he declares that he wants to start his education over again and become "a doctor." This irrational decision, which is built on the old fantasy and union with mother, is so compulsive that it is hard either to influence or to change it. Longing for the mother and the invasion of guilt can supply the beginning of a severe neurosis.

THE ALIENATED

Let us now return to more general problems of adolescence. In the analysis of many brilliant students, it seemed at first that their problems had emerged—*after a normal, hopeful adolescence*—under the impact of later disappointments. According to my observations, however, this was not always the case. The narcissistic attitude that had been present from the start was apparently more vulnerable in adolescence.

The traumatic aspects of adolescence do not leave these brilliant boys with their dreams of glory; instead, some of them go through a period of depressive mood and increased anxiety. Upon their being confronted, however, with the benevolent, active assistance of elements in the new environment, and with a promise of success, the situation of the admiring mother and her aspiring son is restored—and, with it, the narcissistic dream of glory. In these instances, it is the capacity for sublimation that proves to be decisive. For other boys of this type, however, events in adolescence constitute danger signals. They may become very active socially, joining various intellectual groups and being constantly on the go. The defensive role of these pseudo object relationships is clear.

There are other individual variations of the narcissistic types described above. What they appear to have in common is certain environmental circumstances during childhood: these people grew up in an atmosphere that affected their personality structure by increasing and prolonging—with the mother's collaboration—their infantile narcissism.

A certain similarity in regard to the genesis and development of their personality can be found in "the alienated"—a psychological entity described by Kenneth Keniston (1965) in his book *The Uncommitted*. (Through this work, as well as the earlier work by David Riesman [1950]), the "alienated" personality has gained great popularity in the recent literature and in the thinking of the general public. His numbers seem to be increasing in our society, and especially in the colleges. I myself have had the opportunity to see more and more "alienated" personalities, under various social circumstances, and not only in the prestige colleges.)

The fundamental difference between the alienated and the narcissistic types described above lies in their relationship to the external world; it is their socialization that is different. They too have been traumatized by their mothers' excessive devotion to and huge emotional investment in their sons, who will some day—they hope—compensate for their own disappointments and frustrations. The usual identification with the father suffers, as early as during childhood, the typical fate under these circumstances: he is rejected and devalued by the son. This ominous situation is reinforced during adolescence. We have already discussed the danger of devaluation of the father during that period. Keniston's protagonist, Inburn, considers his father to be "much of a failure

in his own eyes"—a debased, devalued, inconsequential figure. The chief reason—not fully conscious—for the boy's re-
sentment against his father is the fact that the latter was too
weak to protect the boy against dependency upon the mother,
and against the boy's incestuous bond with her. The result
of this relationship to the father is that all other men suffer
the same fate at the boy's hands: they too are ridiculed, regarded as weak and worthless. The devaluation of father,
already nurtured during childhood, erupts during adolescence, however, in a dangerous way. It spreads to the whole
new environment, to the entire society: in attacking and
criticizing society, such an adolescent is at bottom attacking
his own father and all that his father stands for.

Let us not forget the general psychological situation in
adolescence. The emotional turmoil of this period certainly
influences *eo ipso* the boy's attitude toward his environment.
The alienated person was, from his childhood on, limited in
his human relationships and in his acceptance of the values
of reality. The new world of which he is now supposed to be
a part is the *man's* world, the world of his father. He refuses
to identify with the father—so important in adolescence—
and thereby rejects *all* social commitments, *all* conventional
values, *all* responsibilities, and *all* emotional closeness with
others. He thus becomes narcissistically preoccupied with his
inner problems. Why is he uncommitted? Because he is
overcommitted—to himself!

As to the sociological background of the alienated: the
subject of Keniston's observations usually comes from a
higher middle-class, often an intellectual family. It is the
father who is here the guiding spirit in the plans and the
aspirations of his son's adolescence. Harvard was the peak of
the father's ambitious dreams, and it is the son who will
bring about their realization. The prestige college—the highest goal of gifted and ambitious students—is expected to
become also the goal of the alienated.

To be a student at Harvard, that prestige institution, is a

prize in itself. The lucky adolescent is thereby presented not only with a glorious *now,* but also with the assurance that, through his becoming a part of that distinguished sector of society, his future is assured. Not only will he participate in cultural progress; he will also be one of those who create it. Keniston therefore believes that the "alienated" is what he is, in spite of the altogether favorable climate and conditions of his existence. On the contrary, I think that this ideal "prestige" world, *by virtue of its social glory, provokes and mobilizes the "alienated's" asocial reactions and his rejection of social values.*

This ideal world is the highest goal of his parents, the father's dream of his son's position in society, and in adolescent rebellion, it is specifically against that world that the adolescent is protesting. He rejects it in an attempt to devalue everything that may be described as "paternal." His intelligence and interests are capable of making him an excellent student—but only on condition that he learns and develops, *not* that he becomes a member and supporter of the prestige society of Harvard.

I know gifted students in colleges of various standing. For them to have been accepted, to be a student at such-and-such college, is also a matter of elevation, prestige, pride and glory —in short, the realization of their parents' dreams. They are alienated to some extent by the very same psychological process as held for the Harvard students. The alienated thus proves to be one among many contemporary adolescents: brilliant, gifted, intellectually outstanding—but emotionally empty, lonely, isolated.

I have given the alienated this much space because I think he is becoming, in increasing numbers, a very important phenomenon of our late adolescents' psychosociological life. But I have also known cultural environments that have differed from those of the contemporary American scene, and yet have harbored alienated people who are identical in character with our present-day "alienated."

I offer a few examples:

1. Russian nihilists, during the decades before the great October Revolution;

2. Adolescents who were deeply involved in the then new Nietzschean philosophy of the "devaluation of all values";

3. From the local scene of my childhood, I remember people who were known as "geniuses without portfolio" (after the hero of a novel). They were people of unusual intelligence and high cultural level; yet their education—for the most part self-acquired—was not utilized toward the attainment of any other goals than self-enrichment.

In all these cases, which I myself have been able to observe directly, it has become evident to me that the mother was the main reason for the son's development. This kind of mother seems to be on the increase. I do not mean the dangerously aggressive type of mother who is popular in this country, and who should be recognized more for her negative, castrating qualities. I am rather applying Erikson's (1950) characterization of "mothers who took the dominant place in the family in the field of education and in cultural life . . . as the fathers abdicated." This seems to be part of the pattern in our society, in which competition is more and more centered on "higher education," college graduation, intellectual pursuits —and the necessarily concomitant curtailment of emotional values.

The alienated suffer not only in the development of their characterological personality; they are usually neurotically sick. Yet a definite clinical diagnosis is seldom possible: they are obsessional, depressive, schizoid. Attempts at psychoanalytic reconstruction of the "alienated" entity are obscured by the additional pathology.

I have seen in consultation quite a number of very gifted boys, whose reaction to the advent of adolescence resulted in rather severe pathology. In my more social and personal encounters with brilliant students, I have learned that their own image of themselves—their conscious ego ideal—is that of pure intellect, unencumbered by emotional influences. The book that they quote, as though it were their Bible, is Freud's *The Future of an Illusion;* they consider themselves to be the representatives of an emerging society, in which reason and logic will be the guiding forces. Their alienation is supposed to be proof of the victory of the critical mind over emotional involvements. My reaction to these brilliant, intellectual personalities is: their blessing is their talent; their curse lies in the impoverishment of their capacity to love.

Fortunately, the union between mother and son is not always as ambiguous in its results as I have shown it to be in the cases presented. Biographies and autobiographies of famous men often show us the immense positive value of such a relationship to mother. But in these cases the binding spirit was not the mother's own narcissistic ambition, nor was it her subsequent idolization of the brilliant child. Ideals of a cultural and aesthetic nature, along with more impersonal goals, have unburdened this relationship, to a great extent, of the narcissistic elements in the son's personality. The mother's love and her belief in the son's future are then able instead to enrich the son's emotional capacity and, at the same time, inspire his creativity. A beautiful example of such a fruitful relationship between mother and son is St. Augustine's relationship to his mother Monica (Rochlin, 1965).

I have already indicated my impression that, in those narcissistic adolescents who have been presented in this study, the oedipus complex did not seem to play its usual powerful role. On looking analytically into the childhood history of these young men, we do not see clearly hatred for the rival; masculine identification with him; strong incestuous wishes or, later, the changes that result from resolution of the oedipus complex. All these are no doubt present—but they are lacking in their usual decisive quality.

Can one then assume that this early union with the mother, the conviction of being the object of her greatest love and admiration—in short, the preoedipal relationship to mother —has actually deprived the oedipus complex of its dynamic power? Does one also have to take into consideration here the father's personality, and especially his failure to create the traditional image of strength and power? We do not yet know; only further psychoanalytic observations will bring answers to these still unanswered questions.

P. Blos (1958) has discussed the other, the negative side of the boy's preoedipal relationship to the mother: "In the preadolescent phase of male puberty, castration anxiety is related to the phallic mother." This horror is reinforced by the fact that the mother is not only castrating but also *seducing*. In either case, she is the dangerous witch, who has to be eluded by way of homosexual defenses.

FEAR OF LONELINESS

The presentation of these cases could not avoid a certain schematization. While they are only one sector of contemporary adolescence, they have meaning with regard to the vast majority of young people, who, for all that they are well adjusted and well functioning, nevertheless also complain about more or less desperate feelings of loneliness.

It was my deeply painful experience to have to listen to their complaints. I have already discussed these feelings as a tragic expression on the part of "geniuses" whose special talent consumed, like a Moloch, their entire emotional life. I have also known those who have had to sacrifice their talent in order to rescue their existence as human beings, and to escape from their painful loneliness (George). The reason why Arnold did not complain was that he *wanted* to stay alone and not to be interfered with by others. By contrast, many brilliant boys wanted to be surrounded by admirers, while the alienated, on the other hand, rejected any external attack on his social disengagement.

Many adolescents who are regarded as completely normal are actually in constant search of a remedy for their feelings of loneliness. Some try to find that remedy in social activities, others in more individual relationships; both attempts may bring only temporary relief.

My limited experience with drug addicts leads me to suspect that their addiction too is often an effort to lessen the pain of this emotional deprivation. Specifically, marihuana seems to be a "companionship" drug *par excellence*. It is striking how seldom the individual smokes "pot" alone, how often he is engaged in the kind of enterprise that is designed to make associates.

These feelings of loneliness are not, however, a prerogative of adolescents; they seem to be a more general evil of our time. Sociologists regard this phenomenon as culturally determined, but a psychoanalyst tries, and is often able, to retrace such subjective feelings to the developmental past. Generally, he finds that this feeling of, and intolerance to, loneliness is the result of a *fear of being alone,* on the part of people whose capacity for object relationship is in some sense impaired. Some of these people are intolerant even of temporary aloneness: their narcissism is in danger, if there are no people around them, confirming by their sheer presence their readiness to love and admire them. Others are afraid of the awakening of their own aggressiveness, and therefore call on other people to facilitate the mobilization of positive feelings in themselves. In still other cases, these are people who simply need the noise of entertainment for distraction.

I am here differentiating "isolation" from the sensation of loneliness. Creative people generally need isolation in order to be creative. In speaking of "geniuses," I have already emphasized their struggle between creativity and the ability to tolerate isolation. On the other hand, isolation in adolescence may also prove to be the precursor of a psychotic illness. In the important work that has been done by M. Katan (1954, 1958), we find clinical material dealing with these problems.

Many suffer the worst form of loneliness; these are the ones who are not able to communicate their feelings on that score. This is extremely common among adolescents, who may share their secrets, but not their most painful sensation—that of loneliness. Only after they have reached a certain degree of positive transference is one able to see how lonely and how deprived of emotional experiences many of our brilliant contemporary youths are! With long experience and after numerous encounters with lonely adolescents, I have succeeded in coming a little closer to understanding them. I have learned that this feeling of loneliness is actually a step forward—from narcissistic isolation to a passive stage of longing and expectation. In this passive attitude, there is an element of an inner call for contact, an expression of tension and of a wish to love and be loved. It does not lead to these goals, however, because the inner energy expressed in "I am lonely" is intercepted by narcissistic forces of the ego and utilized—more or less successfully—for narcissistic goals. Those who are not able to communicate thus hide a more severe neurotic disturbance; they can be helped only when an overwelming anxiety finally directs them to treatment.

We have so far discussed late adolescent boys chiefly in terms of their individual problems. Let us not forget, however, that the cultural setting within which the overestimation of intellect replaces social ideologies and intellectualization makes this process not only a defense mechanism of adolescence, but also the central goal of a great part of American society. Higher education is now open to all—to those who are truly capable of dealing with it, as well as to those who become victims of anxiety and frustration because the goal is higher than their capacity.

Even more significant is the downgrading, even by the parents themselves, of any form of productive activity other than that which involves "higher education," both in its preparation and in its execution. "I want my son to do *better than I did*" can often, paradoxically, provide the motive force for ultimately ensuring that that very son will not only do harm to himself in straining to reach a purported "better" for which he is not really equipped, but will also lose the opportunity to do very well, and to be socially quite productive, at those tasks for which he is equipped.

CHAPTER 3

GROUP FORMATION IN ADOLESCENCE

We now return via a detour to some of the sociological aspects of adolescence. The sociopolitical conditions in America in our times have not been such as to encourage the youth to the adoption of programmatic, concrete activity, or to conscious and continuous participation in social events. Their individualistic agitation tended rather to stem from an internal situation on the part of each one, which has become externalized; one way of achieving this has been by way of identification with the underprivileged. The so-called "affluent society" has provided neither the occasion for nor the real focus of attack of the revolutionary ideology of the young. Instead, it has actually supported their wishes by enlarging the scope of their personal freedom, supporting their education, etc.

In previous generations, and especially in European countries, "isms" used to arouse and direct the revolutionary spirit of the younger generation. There are no such inspiring "isms" in our society today and, as a consequence, the majority of contemporary youth in the United States have remained politically aloof. Their strivings and ambitions have therefore had an orientation that is much more personal than social. All adolescent groups share the core attitude of rebellion and of the search for a refuge from anxiety. Their emphasis lies in such feelings as: *"Alone* I am lost; *together* we

69

are strong. It is the 'we' that gives me the feeling of social identity and thereby safeguards me against anxiety."

Since adolescence is above all characterized by the fact that, in the complex process of maturation, various progressive and regressive forces appear at the same time, the individual character, as well as the different forms of acting out, that are manifested in group formations will of course be manifold. For example, where it is the intensification of aggressiveness that is dominant, the groups that will attract these adolescents are the ones that present an outlet for their aggressiveness. If the superego is mobilized by the reappearance of old feelings of guilt—now reinforced by new guilt feelings—the aggression may turn these feelings against the self. The acting out will then have a more decidedly masochistic character, which may take either a socially valuable form or, by contrast, a harmful turn against the ego. How often it is that a youth who, until then, has been well adjusted and even singularly "good," to everyone's surprise commits a delinquent act! He seldom does so individually; more often, he has joined a delinquent group—but as no more than a passing fancy, since, with the progress of maturity, delinquent tendencies usually subside. The end of this sequence of events may be the punishment that was, from the start, the unconscious goal of the asocial acting out.

In regard to all juvenile groups, we assume the existence— overt, concealed, or unconscious—of a protest by the young generation against the preceding one. Nevertheless, the modes of expressing this protest will be different for different groups, and we may find identical motivations at the bottom of organizations of delinquents and of highly idealistic revolutionary groups. Since groups are aggregations of individuals, the goals and the level of the group will be determined in large part by the kind of individuals they include.

I start with a group that appears to be numerically the most popular. The streets of big American cities, as well as of a great many small communities, swarm with odd-looking adolescents of both sexes. The attire of the boys is like a uniform: dirty black (or blue) jeans, fitted tightly to their (usually thin) legs; dirty, always open jackets; long hair, long enough to hang over the neck; and a very characteristic hair-do, with sideburns. With these, they arrive at a very great similarity in appearance, so that one is hardly able to distinguish one from the other. This appearance, along with their entire concomitant behavior, they think of as a kind of great adventure; instead, it is a childish acting out—without imagination, and without offering any proof of either courage or individuality. All they really do is imitate each other, until a complete conforming "we" has been achieved.

The reaction of the people around them is quite interesting. More mature people become irritated with their showiness and their mannerisms—above all, with the standardization of their atttiudes, and the fact that they regard themselves as original and different, at the very time when their most striking feature is actually their self-imitation: one of them exactly like another.

If one asks them about the reasons for this uniformity, one always gets the same explanation: "Everybody is doing it," or "This is our business, not yours"—with a gesture of superiority, as if to say: "*This* is the *new* world. . . ." Yet the absence of any real activity or courage in this sort of performance is so obvious that one cannot even attempt to ascribe it to an abundance of sexual energy—at that age biologically intensified, although usually not yet goal-directed.

If one is less than tolerant—as the majority of people are— one is tempted to think of their "uniform" as being designed, more or less consciously, to conceal their lack of betters ways in which to express what is no more than a feeling of rebelliousness. They are *playing* at being independent, free, "different": their entire mode of existence shows no real signs of moving forward, maturing. They aspire to be "original," and yet at the same time they hanker to achieve the greatest degree of conformity possible with thousands of their fellow adolescents. In this search for conformity lies the most important motive of such adolescent group formation: peer identity!

One may call this uniformed masquerade: "identity card: *we*," and assume that it serves—as do so many other expressions in adolescent life—to hide their *anxiety,* and to keep it under control. The revolutionary protest expresses itself in simply being "different from"—*the older generation!*

It is understandable, therefore, that the psychological atmosphere in this group should be not very inspiring—barren as it is of any other leadership or goals than the satisfaction of being one part of a large body of individuals who are thus identified by negation. What gives the individuals involved a feeling of gratification is precisely the numerical largeness of the group, the sense of importance they derive from the noisy emphasis (even if it is negative) on their existence.

A further gratification for the adolescents is their new-found freedom of action: what individually they would not dare to do, they can permit themselves to do under the protective aegis of their numerical superiority. In short, gratification for the members of this group lies paradoxically in the "self-assertion" they achieve through *the repudiation of their own individuality and their acceptance of identity with others.*

This is indeed a peer society—but without any other goals than the "search for identity." It is their anticipation of an angry reaction on the part of society that gives to the members of this adolescent community a feeling of revolutionary importance and even, in a sense, of achievement. The feeling of identity that they share with the numberless other members of the group is so strong that even critical members are not shocked or embarrassed by the fact that they conform to such a high degree that they all look alike!

Many exhibitionistic acts of the "group" betray the fact that these acts function as defenses against, or gratifications of, once frustrated and never since satisfied strivings of the past. For example, the notorious dirtiness of the group members is so widespread that it impresses the milieu as being, in effect, a group rule: what it demonstrates is the adolescent's triumph over the previously enforced cleanliness of childhood. Apparently, cleanliness had remained associated with submission to the social order of childhood; in adolescence, it is rejected in the very gesture of rebellion. Identification now has to do with the regressive revival of the pregenital past.

Another example of peer identification, which stemmed from the revival of direct active gratification of the anal residue of the past, could be seen in the changing attitude of a gifted college student who began by being interested in classical literature and was at that time considered by his instructors to be a promising member of the academic community. In this capacity, he had already achieved a certain identity, in which he could feel secure and recognized. I do not know what sort of experience it was that interfered with his further development along these lines, but the turmoil of adolescence now sharply redirected his talents. He joined a group of unsophisticated "friends," of a much lower intellectual and social status than he, and with them cultivated a "dirty" and debased kind of existence, in which he used his writing talent for pornographic literary activity.

In this instance, apparently, not only was a strong regressive force able to deprive him of his previously successful sublimations, but his inherent need for identification was able to find an outlet in a low-grade group formation. Such group formations are usually rooted in earlier adolescence, in which the externalization of inner tension—the acting out—is characteristic.[1]

This need for identification with peers is of the greatest importance among some adolescents. The youth who later reach identity via more desirable routes do not need this masquerade. I have observed that many boys begin to dress more

[1] For a recent survey of the concept of acting out as well as of problems of acting out in childhood and adolescence, see Rexford (1966).

conventionally, change their hairdo "a little bit," etc., on the day when their coveted college acceptance notification arrives. The masquerade seems no longer to be needed; it begins to fall away, once real "status" has been reached. Apparently, after the earlier and more primitive form of "revolution," it has become clearer to them how to get where one has all along really wanted to: by trying to become a successful citizen, perhaps even a better one than father has been. What happened earlier, then, was a "revolution without a cause."

In short, the preceding rebelliousness did not constitute a real social upheaval of the youth. It was rather a refuge from anxiety; an infantile declaration in favor of freedom and individuality; an attempt to be a different "I"—that is, to be like the mass of one's peers and to feel oneself to be important by way of the attention that is given to them all: *"the adolescents."*

Since this group of adolescents is, however, numerically the largest—not only in America, but also in other countries— one must assume that it includes a variety of individuals, who are distinct from one another in regard to their upbringing, cultural interests, social background, etc. Moreover, it seems to take in all those who, without embracing any of the contemporary ideologies, have felt a need for the conformity of the "we."

One may be inclined to regard this primitive group formation as a kind of childhood disease that will pass with time, without any further consequences. Unfortunately, there is one element involved that may be of really lasting consequence—the rebellious demand for sexual freedom and the tendency to an indiscriminate use of that freedom. It is one of the contemporary misconceptions that biological development is identical with psychological maturity! I regard this so-called "freedom," along with the trend toward uninhibited sexual activity, as demonstrating no real progress at all nor as offering any advantage toward further emotional maturation.

The most striking mass expression of this trend is in the direction of bisexuality. What makes the observer doubtful about its meaning is a certain contradiction in the whole behavior. Can it be that a young man who has only recently been inaugurated into his manhood and is fighting for recognition as a man would really choose publicly and noisily to deny his masculinity? Is the predisposition to bisexuality actually so powerful in adolescence that it is able to proclaim its presence, even in the midst of a psychological atmosphere of "Now I am a man"?

Predisposition alone does not seem to provide an answer to that question. My own direct observations of a number of boys have convinced me that they are fearful of various vicissitudes in their forthcoming development. The fear of not being able to be "real" men, after all, makes them deny their actual efforts in this diretcion. Their additional anxiety is that the achievement of their masculinity will involve them once again in struggles with the oedipus complex, which they want to escape. And, above all, it is their horror of their own aggressive impulses, which are connected in their minds with masculinity, that gives rise to their attempt to withdrawn into a protective "femininity."

I believe that another very real element is responsible for the male adolescent's attire. We have not yet fully emerged from the "Beatle" era. Imitation of these heroes certainly contributed, at least at the start, to the "social movement"—that is, to the external expression of "femininity" as part of "the adolescent revolution." In this "lamb's wool," the aggressiveness of the boys has acquired a certain freedom of action: never before has sexual activity in early adolescence been so generally accepted as it has been by this generation; never has the relationship to the other sex been so goal-directed, so barren of any tenderness or adoration—in short, of the glorification of love. The general assumption that boys are now more feminine is thus a gross error, inspired mainly by the boys' external behavior. Except in cases of manifest homosexuality, a boy would never expose his femininity directly and openly, if it were not for the purpose of serving certain indirect psychological motives.

On the other hand, early sexual gratification seems to hold no advantages whatsoever for emotional maturity.[2] As far as the solution of the oedipus complex is concerned, this form of running away is also not the best method. It made a very unpleasant effect on me to hear these boys speaking with disrespect of their female companions, in the framework of what they call "social progress." Nevertheless, I was aware that by and by they would choose one of two ways of functioning: either turning to a more individualistic mode of existence, or else joining another group, this time, however, with more definite and more mature goals, in terms of which their attitude toward their female companions would also change.

IDENTITY BETWEEN BOYS AND GIRLS

I now turn to a very popular subgroup, whose task seems to be the declaration of sexual identity between boys and girls. This emphasis on identity between the sexes is overtly expressed in their attire, behavior, etc. They appear in pairs, for example, on the streets and in public places—especially in London and Stockholm, but also in other European cities, and more sporadically in America.

The apparent intention of this "new look" is to obliterate the external differences between the sexes. This is achieved successfully: the appearance of boys and girls is so nearly identical that it is often well-nigh impossible to recognize which is a boy and which a girl. Their clothing is completely the same; both have long hair, falling loose over the shoulder; even their gait and body movements are strikingly similar.

In this oneness of the sexes, however, it is quite clear that the boy is the dominant figure. The girl seems to be willing to yield her feminine identity to the boy and to accept his

---

[2] See Chapter 4 on the adolescence of girls.

orders willingly and submissively. According to the fashion experts, for example, the designers and tailors work first on the boys' clothing, and then repeat the attire in complete facsimile in the feminine department. They all emphasize the fact that the fashion is inspired by the boys and effected primarily for the boys, the girls being only a kind of supplementary passive "double."

There have been many attempts to explain this curious phenomenon. Sociologists pose their theories in terms of specifically sociological elements; psychologists and psychiatrists present various speculations, based mainly on the "adolescent rebellion." Britain, which has been troubled for years with homosexuality, and Sweden, which is faced with a rising wave of it, see a connection between homosexuality and the cult of being alike. The gross business interest of the clothing industry, on the other hand, makes the exhibitionistic performance a lucrative fashion; the young people themselves do not know the reason behind the fashion, binding as it is. They may attempt some superficial and feeble rationalization, apparently unaware that their grotesque appearance is an acting out—an effort to realize unconscious fantasies.

THE BISEXUAL FANTASY AND IMMORTALITY

The question has thus remained unanswered so far. Why do the adolescents—both boys and girls, and perhaps the former more than the latter—want to look alike and to deny, by way of their attire, the differences between the sexes? In searching for an answer, I took as my point of departure the psychological situation of the adolescent: his inner preoccupation with himself; his uncertainty about his goals; his narcissism, and his dreams of achievement and glory; and, finally, and perhaps most important, the increased tension produced by his anxieties. Whenever one has the opportunity to gain analytic insight into the anxieties of adolescents, one is struck by their preoccupation with death; in many instances, even castration anxiety becomes dissolved in the more overwhelming threats of annihilation.

A letter written by Freud to a friend[3] after his *abitur* or *matura,* which is equivalent to the American college-entrance examination, expresses his own tension-laden expectation of accomplishing outstanding things in the future. He advises the friend, jokingly, to keep his letters—"take good care of them, bind them"—because "one can never know. . . ." He also confides to this friend his worries about the future, his doubts and his hopes. One has the feeling that here was a dream of future greatness, at that time still less than fully rational, and at the same time connected with a fearful uncertainty about the possibility of its achievement. The fulfillment of Freud's adolescent fantasies in his later life proved them to have been prophetic. But they are not altogether different from the fantasies of many intelligent adolescent boys, who are not, as Freud was, marked for future greatness.

When one bears in mind that the adolescent struggles with intense anxiety, confronted as he is with one of life's sharpest paradoxes—namely, that on the threshold of a new life, he also feels the threat of death[4]—one has little difficulty in recognizing that many adolescent activities are indeed expressions of this anxiety and of the defenses instituted against it. There are various ways of conquering this specific anxiety: at one extreme real achievements; at the other, flight into fantasies. Either fame and immortality of an earthly character, or else eternal life: the attainment of immortality by way of death.

Among those who are believers, the desire for immortality is fulfilled by religious beliefs. A Catholic priest, Father X., a man who is endowed with a superior and critical mind, told me how, in his work, especially with juveniles, he is often impelled to think: "What are people, especially young peo-

3 Letter to Emil Fluss, 1873.
4 One sees this proximity of life and death also in emotional experiences of pregnancy (H. Deutsch, 1945).

ple, in their great anxieties doing without this belief? What substitute are you offering them?"

I was somewhat embarrassed by this question because I am aware that the appeal to rationality, along with the intellectual orientation that rejects any possibility of life after death, cannot find any hold in the turbulent inner life of the adolescent. Tormented by anxiety, he will seek consolation and refuge in his fantasies, protecting himself from the horrors of death by the illusion of an eternal continuity of life. By way of regression, he will reawaken old childhood stories and myths and attach these to his knowledge of biological facts. With regard to the desire for immortality, there is an abundance of material produced by adolescents that provides a clear insight into their concerns and hopes; their dreams and poetry; and their conscious and unconscious fantasies, which are communicated either directly or indirectly, etc. Their ways of trying to reach immortality are more hidden; any attempt to elucidate them must stay within the limits of the speculations that can be based on our general knowledge of adolescence.

I was fascinated to hear a group of high school students discussing with intensity a lecture that had been delivered in their school by a noted biologist. He spoke about the self-propagation of certain organisms and demonstrated to the young enthusiasts the existence of a biological process that really leads to immortality—by way of the propagation of oneself *without partnership*. Being quite clever, these young scientists developed in their conversation a theory of bisexuality, as the way to the realization of immortality via the self-propagation of *homo sapiens*.

This biologically oriented speculation would appear to have its analogy in a deeply rooted fantasy of adolescents, which thus seems to be, after all, the guiding spirit behind the boy-girl identity. Double-sexed unity is the way to achieve bisexuality and, with it, the ultimate goal of immortality. The grotesque denial of sex differences is an expression of the boys' own feminine fantasies, by projection onto an external object and, at the same time, an identification with this object, in a kind of mirror-twin fantasy. It is like a realization of the myth of Narcissus who, upon looking into the mirror of river water, sees the image of his twin sister. The boy's fear of women is conquered by his making the girl into a boy, while, on the other hand, homosexuality is ruled out by the actual sex of this love partner ("she is my chick").

The bisexual fantasy seems also to be present in a more individual form: the bearded man with long hair, who expresses in his own body the desire to be both woman and man. The "beatnik" often refers to the past as the source of his form of identification. He is right: in various periods of cultural development, there has appeared the bearded man with long hair: some of Shakespeare's heroes, for example, or the figures of the Bible, etc. The appearance and disappearance of this external expression runs like a red thread through the history of mankind. Whatever the level of psychological understanding that may be attained with regard to the historical past, our adolescents' external expression of their inner processes enables us to employ a more direct, objective approach. In his gross rejection of society, in his self-created dissociation and loneliness, the beatnik cries out, through his external appearance: "*I* am. I do not need society: I do not need another human creature, because I am both man and woman in myself."

I was surprised to see, in museums of ancient art, our beatniks in classic form, or at least prototypes of them of a striking similarity: Dionysus, the god of joy and happiness, of wine and ecstatic bacchanals, "the god who by very simple means enables you for a short time to stop being yourself and thereby sets you free. The individual began in that age to emerge for the first time from the old solidarity of the family and found the unfamiliar burden of individual responsibility hard to bear. Dionysus could lift it from him" (Dodds, 1951, p. 76f.).

The following is taken from C. Kerenyi's *The Gods of the Greeks* (1951): "The surnames of Dionysus only seldom describe the god as the 'phallic one,' but on the rare occasions when this aspect of him is openly mentioned, the names plainly have an extensive, although perhaps not complete, common identity: such names as *Orthos,* 'the erect', *Enorches,* the 'betesticled'. . . . On the other hand, he was also called *Pseudanor,* 'the man without virility', and such joking names as *gynnis* 'the womanish,' or *arse-nothelys* 'the man-womanly.'" These surnames, Kerenyi believes, are derived from tales of the God's bisexuality (p. 273).

Other surnames, *Dendites, Endendros,* "the treegod" or "the one in the tree," or names connected with vegetable luxuriance and growth, such as *Phleon, Phleus,* or *Phloios,* indicate that "what is meant is not a human sexual hybridity, but the bisexuality that is characteristic of most trees and in fact constitutes their natural completeness" (Kerenyi). This completeness has to do with propagation: the identity of Dionysus with trees is by way of his bisexuality and the production of offspring by himself (as trees do).

In many myths and rituals, immortality signifies rebirth through renewal and transformation. One of the ways in which to gain renewal of life is by way of the bisexual character of the individual who acquires immortality through self-propagation. In the study of the myth of Dionysus, with regard to his struggle for immortality, one becomes aware that it expresses a more human need for immortality.

In woman this is met with in various versions of parthenogenetic fantasies of producing a child without the participation of the male sex, "as a maiden," by oneself. But the parthenogenetic fantasy seems to emphasize the total exclusion of sex, whereas immortality fantasies seek only to exclude partnership as the condition of one's own bisexual existence.

To impose the ideas of immortality on the activities of fun-loving adolescents may seem like mere speculation—and over-serious, at that. In fact, however, it is a knowledge that is acquired again and again in clinical observations and confirmed in many of the literary productions by adolescents.[5] We can understand that, in the period in which all inner forces are reinforced, so too is this need, which is common to all. Ideas of immortality, which are later to be lost in mature life, to be rejected along with myths and religious beliefs, are, according to my observations, strongly reawakened during the troubled years of adolescence.

Much attention is now being paid to the growing child's reactions to separation and the loss of objects, to his griefs and anxieties.[6] In adolescence, immortality is not only the denial of death and annihilation, but also an expression of the wish to be famous—immortal by way of achievement, as well as by way of conquest of the biological restrictions on propagation. It is these deeply rooted childhood fantasies that have been finding their external expression, among other ways, in the boy-girl masquerade of today's adolescents.

The loss of childhood rights and gratifications; the uncertainty of the next refuge that is available to him for his "deserted" yet still deeply dependent existence; the sense that now he has to prove himself as a grown-up member of society; and, finally, the ominous feeling of loneliness—all these serve to direct the young person away from the anxiety-laden "I" into the more secure "we" of a group of peers. As a protective measure against the anxieties of the juvenile "I," the "we" takes on the character of a counterphobic refuge. This is especially true during the earlier period of adolescence, but to some degree it accompanies the entire process of maturation.

The "we" may draw its power from a purely numerical superiority (as in the primitive gangs described above), or else it may lead to the formation of groups of a specific char-

[5] One also encounters the delusion of bisexuality and of self-propagation in the schizophrenia of adolescents.

[6] In his *Griefs and Discontents* (1965), G. Rochlin discusses in a scholarly fashion the problem of immortality. His ideas and the material presented in the book have stimulated my hypothesis.

acter. Some are based directly on the emotional needs of youth. Their goal is purely pleasure: dances, record-listening, auto rides—in short, "happy youth," as they might perhaps be called. Unfortunately, they are not always happy. Often they look for fun only as a way of being together with others and in order to avoid loneliness.

SEXUAL FREEDOM

Another group formation that is based primarily on personal needs and customs and not on social ideologies takes place in later adolescence, within the academic framework. It reflects the coeducational setting, in that it generally consists of three to five pairs of co-eds, who meet regularly and spend all their free time together. The pairing in this group usually follows sexual attraction, and is more or less active in that direction. Whether this is really an expression of sexual needs, or simply a demonstration of sexual freedom, is hard to tell. In these groups, sexual activity is seldom an expression of rebellion as it was, primarily, in early adolescence. There are indications that these are rather the modern demands of an older generation that want to free the youth in aspects of life in which they themselves were subject to restriction.

The young people are not always ready for it, yet they feel a kind of obligation to uphold the new aspect of freedom. This modernization, which apparently does not arise out of any real need or conviction, is one of the most interesting and paradoxical problems of the modern adolescent situation. In some of these groups, the spirit of identification is so strong that, should one of its members actually demonstrate an unwillingness to comply with the demands of sexual freedom (as happens quite often), the rest of the group then stigmatizes the hesitant individual as "abnormal" and "in need of psychoanalysis." (See Chapter 4.)

Further development in socialization will depend on the success of sublimations and the progress of adaptation; on

acceptance of identity and on the interplay between narcissism and the capacity to relate to other individuals.

Has the maturing individual developed enough activity to
lay aside his aggressiveness? Has he stabilized his relationships
with others through the acceptance of certain general social
values, or has that stabilization been carried through in
accordance with his own personal interests and goals? Does
he join "the others" in order to escape loneliness, or out of
the need to be accepted and admired? Has he made his way
to freedom through a hostility against his family that is now
extended to society? Is his attitude toward the world one of
passive dependency, or is he ready to deal with external reality actively? Does he join new peer groups in the name of
ideological values or in order to perform delinquent acts?

Whatever may be the forms and ostensible aims of adolescent group formations, the psychological motivation of the
adolescent is above all to achieve his freedom by escaping
from childhood. At the same time, he is confronted with the
unknown forces of the future. The desire to find one's own
path is mixed with the terrible fear of failing in that quest—
which may very well happen if there is no definite goal to
help the adolescent hold his own against pressures, not only
from the past, but also from the future. Adolescents have
traditionally protested against the social order, yet their attempts to change it are, for obvious reasons, nowhere near
strong enough. As a result, they are often reduced to protesting against conventions and habits, without being able to
propose anything better with which to replace them. For
adolescents as a whole, their protest helps to condition their
growth; but, for many, it is only a *feu·d'artifice*, without any
real consequences either for them or for the society against
which they are supposedly rebelling.

Many are hampered by their own intellectual control and
self-criticism, which may very well prove to be stronger than
their criticism of society. Some project their own self-devalua-
tion onto the outside world, thus trying to change themselves

by way of changes in society. Some, under the pressure of obsessional traits in their own personality, surrender to their personal need for peace and balance; they thus withdraw from any participation at all in social upheaval. By contrast, there are those who carry out their social protests in a rather childish kind of disobedience—a simple refusal to do what is expected of them.

To understand adolescents requires therefore that one be capable of understanding their inconsistencies, and their often seemingly quite senseless activities. From generation to generation the effort is repeated to upset the existing order, to challenge the established equilibrium ("The Establishment") by protest against one's immediate predecessors. The methods and the form of this protest will, of course, vary with the contemporary social situation.

Wherever adolescent group activities develop, there are individual personalities around whom the leadership of these activities centers. Sometimes their power to influence is of the greatest importance; but, in most of the contemporary youth movements, they are only transient figures, and make no definite or lasting impact on the others. They appear and disappear, without having produced any real or lasting consequences.

SOCIAL IDEOLOGIES

Our contemporary society has recently begun to develop serious social ideologies that can assist in the social growth of this generation. Youth participation in the civil rights movement, in housing reforms, in the first against poverty and in other such social projects seems to offer the adolescent an adequate opportunity to express his identification with the victims of society and in that way to realize his own revolutionary protest. But only a small sector of today's youth as yet participates in these activities, and they cannot serve as the spokesmen for newly created values of a social, political, moral or intellectual character for an entire generation. The group activities of the majority of our youth are very often not the expression of a particular ideology, but—as we have seen all too often—little more than a childish play-acting, a caricature.

The ideological and moral aspect of more serious activities is also often established and maintained through the efforts of persons in authority (school directors, teachers, sometimes even parents). This adult involvement gives the social activity a more "good boy" (or "good girl") aspect, however, so that, even if it is accepted by the youth with enthusiasm, it seldom proves to be of lasting effect. In the efforts to change the environment, the acquired ideology itself becomes a part of the past and is rejected. This can be observed with particular clarity after students leave high school and enter college.

Patronage by the older generation of a youthful revolution is psychologically, in fact, a token of the end of its dynamic power. The ending of this period is sometimes followed by the beginning of a more aggressive revolutionary attitude, or else—depending on the particular personality—of a retreat into a more completely individual form of existence.

What strikes one about the adolescent generation of our time, then, is that the majority of them are idealistic. But they have the tendency to turn *toward reality:* their goals then become grossly realistic and concrete, and the more subjective emotional elements make their appearance only in acute explosive actions.

Even if their demands sometimes seem irrational, however, once they have been brought into a sociological focus, they will be found to be based on a well-defined reality; they are not at all exotic or farfetched. The political group activities of adolescents may even be quite traditional; when there is a call for moderation on the part of the authorities, it is not essentially because adolescent activities are truly revolutionary—that is to say, directed against the foundations of society. As far as youth groups are concerned, the intervention of authorities is usually not directed against their goals so much as it is against their intensity and their provocative attitude. By the same token, however, behind the ostensibly moderate and rational external goal, there actually does lie an *inner* revolution, which is what really calls forth the reaction of the authorities.

Participation in the activities of already organized and belligerent groups (for example, those involved in civil rights) is a classic instance of identification with the underdog—a very important psychological motivation that is typical of adolescence.

There is no doubt that, among the senior adolescents in America today, there is a trend toward the organization of groups that function independently of mere second-class participation in already organized social activities. They seek to emerge directly from the status of adolescence into the status of "grownups." There are probably no Georges, Arnolds, "Nobel Prize winners" or "alienated" among them. This does not mean, however, that narcissistic or isolated individuals are not among them, searching for ways to get out of their loneliness by "joining."

A research coordinator in the Institute for the Study of Human Problems, Joseph Katz (1965), in reporting his preliminary findings of five years of study (including a study of Berkeley), has remarked that "For all the campus demonstrations, the average American college student is as docile and conformist as ever. And he has just as tight a hold on mother's apron strings." According to various reports, "the occupational and marital choices of most students, and even their fundamental ideologies, have stayed close to parental wishes and beliefs . . . these unseen strings, behind the appearance of encouraging independence and self-determination, help create personalities . . . to depend on what others think. Data from questionnaires and personal interviews at Berkeley and Stanford revealed a strongly 'privatist' orientation among students. They rank highest their own individual careers. . . .

Involvement in international, national, or civic affairs . . . are
ranked astonishingly low." Some investigators put the blame
on the colleges which, while they preach independence, in
their teaching methods actually press for passivity and accept-
ability, as the shortest and surest way to grades and honors.

What has the psychoanalyst, as an objective psychological
observer, to say about all this?

When we look more closely into the events a while back
at Berkeley, we find confirmation of the fact that the not yet
completed struggles of adolescence still play their part in this
process of liberation. Behind the only to be welcomed struggle
for self-determination and the encouraging signs of effective
independence, we find the forces of adolescence in action.
They are aiming, as before, toward their resolution, but on a
higher level, consonant with their activity and endowed with
social values, in a continuing process of maturation.

The demands of the Berkeley students for various freedoms
were, in effect, a continuation and a crystallization of their
more private revolt, of their fight against the restrictions
of their childhood environment. Characteristically, what
brought into being the students' strongly emotional outburst
was the fact that the restrictions on their freedom constituted
a withdrawal of *privileges that had already been granted and
enjoyed*. Well oriented about the political forces at work behind the college's restrictions, each revolting student, and all
of them together, felt that withdrawal to be *an insult against
their advancing maturity and their growing sense of responsibility*. Berkeley was typical of the situation in which the
personal aims of the individuals involved are united in a
"we"—in this case, in the constructive, mature "we" of a
localized upheaval.

At a time when observers have reported that the majority
of students in America are still dependent on their parents'
values, the student movement that was inaugurated at Berkeley must have seen as a very serious and wholly welcome
attempt on the part of maturing students to free themselves

from retarding dependency. It is true that the revolt of the students was centered around purely personal demands, and it was in the name of these demands that the rights of students were fought for. But what a step this was beyond the group activities of those students who had been demanding improvement in the food, better living quarters, and longer hours for entertaining women in dormitories!

Another strongly emphasized demand was for more regular individual contact between students and professors. An analyst cannot but be in agreement with this demand, knowing as he does the need and importance of a father substitute, precisely during the process of the adolescent's emancipation from the father.

Like other aspects of adolescence, however, the student revolution, although it served progressive goals, could not by itself prevent the awakening of regressions. How irritating it must have been, therefore, for serious student activists and their sympathizers to find themselves being joined by groups of noisy boys who, in their anal regression, were demanding the freedom to use dirty words, or others who were gratifying their infantile exhibitionism by their mode of attire, under the slogan of "freedom from modesty"!

The progress from a purely personal "student program" to a more universal ideology was first openly declared in the march—historical in the annals of the University at Berkeley —to Oakland in protest against Vietnam. A Congress in Madison, Wisconsin, September 3, 1965, demonstrated by the presence of nearly one thousand collegians that the trend toward political activism on the campuses was growing. The subjects at this Congress were of general importance: Vietnam, peace, poverty, civil rights, academic freedom. The resolutions were extremely radical, which only corroborates the fact that the *real* actions of students are on the liberal side, as they always have been in the history of social upheavals.

There are, of course, counterforces among the students

themselves: conservative student groups, which fight against the radicals, and "uncommitted" groups, as objective observers. As a whole, however, the "new left" has seemed to be very much on the march. The uninvolved students are nevertheless still in a large majority. Psychological factors are certainly responsible for this in part, but the interpretation of that situation still has to be the responsibility of the sociologists.

I mentioned previously that the lack of well-defined ideological goals is one of the reasons for the slow development of adolescent social involvement and—connected with it—the absence of great leaders. The leadership of student revolts is usually in the hands of a student himself—a respected and trusted youth, but one who is not necessarily psychologically adequate to the task. One also has the impression that these young *ad hoc* leaders soon disappear from the public scene, following the first wave of enthusiasm.

The recent political situation has also been provoking a regression to self-absorption and anxiety among our youth, who have taken to learning with ardor—as a means of avoiding the draft—meanwhile grinding their teeth in a sort of anguished passivity.

In writing about the youth movements, I earlier remarked, inspired by information from the sociologists and in accordance with my own observations, that whatever we may say about a youth movement, its stability and the continuity of its goals are by no means necessarily assured. This has proven to be true.

A great number of both younger and older adolescents are no longer satisfied with the mere pursuit of their tasks as students; although they are not yet ready for commitment to "causes," they now seem unwilling to accept purely personal ambitions as their goals in life. Thus, they offer their assistance to the implementation of direct and immediate social goals: teaching, housing programs, hospital work, etc. What is important to note, however, is that the activity of these young people no longer has the character of a direct revolutionary protest. They are not attempting to change society, but instead to help in the process of alleviating its most glaring ills. Their role is therefore distinctly that of the social worker, and they are willing to work under the auspices of some higher and even official authority.

This more recent change in attitude is obviously not the expression of any intellectual change with regard to social issues. It is rather another episode in the turmoil of adolescence: a transformation in identity; a search for status; a flight from passivity into activity; and, ultimately, appeasement of the superego. One might even say that this new trend makes the "social worker" youth, paradoxically, the counterparts of those youth who are now more than ever joining antisocial gangs and cliques. These are, after all, merely two different ways, at this juncture, of avoiding the suffering of isolation and of conquering the anxiety that has been so sharply increased by the threat of full-scale war.

For a psychoanalyst, every single act of social activity on the part of adolescents is, in essence, a problem of their development toward maturity—except that the free run of a normal or pathological force is often either directed or rerouted by social necessities and pressures.

In dealing with the psychological problems of contemporary youth as a social group, I have often had to refer to individual cases. Childhood histories—in particular, the mother's role—have provided meaningful evidence of the etiological factors in their developmental problems. We might say that the present generation of adolescents was reared in a kind of matriarchy—an emotional climate that is decisive for the development of children. It is the active role of the mothers that is more responsible for the ambitions and the educational goals of the children than is the father's role. I am speaking here of those large social groups in which higher education is a relatively new thing, and the attitude toward it takes on a *nouveau riche* character.

The postponement of the completion of this monograph has provided me with the opportunity for a larger span of observation and, with it, new insights into the fate of group formations that I described previously. There is not much left these days of the earlier "noise" and "senselessness." What still remains of the demonstratively "revolutionary" attire has since lost its meaning; it is now little more than a fashion.

From the masquerade of identity of much of the previous decade there have emerged a good many individuals with social ideals and new groups, formed in the service of a definite ideology. The danger of military service, which hangs like a dark cloud over the most important developmental years of our youth, is indeed oppressive. Nevertheless, even granted that reactions to the threat of being drafted may have begun as personal fears, youth's protests against the war itself have increasingly taken on a more mature character. The attitude of students to the threatened abolition of their defer- ment has often been—against their own interests—an expres- sion of their protest against the basic injustice of the war.

One cannot say for certain, at this point, what lies ahead. The modest data set forth in this monograph, and the still necessarily tentative hypotheses with which I have sought to interpret those data, may prove, I hope, to be of some useful- ness for an understanding of the avalanche of social and political events with which, at this moment, not only the youth of our society but the society itself is faced.

CHAPTER 4

THE ADOLESCENCE OF GIRLS

In the chapter that follows, as in those that have preceded it, on group formations in adolescence, I shall restrict myself to phenomena of a definitely contemporary character. Here too I want to deal with them as essentially *episodes* within the framework of American society—immediate and even vivid forms of expressions of psychologically meaningful forces, yet so time-bound that, even within the relatively short span of these observations, they have appeared, disappeared, and changed in form and in significance.

To a certain extent, this holds true for the social acts of girls, no less than it did for the adolescent boys with whom we dealt earlier. For adolescent girls, however, their social involvement does not always constitute, in the end, the successful end act of a chain of developmental events. Here the biological difference often finds its most powerful—and unfortunately sometimes disastrous—expression.

In any case, the fight for "equal rights for women" now seems somewhat antiquated in its goals. The long and often quite hard struggle that was carried on by both men and women of past generations did succeed in preparing society —at least in the advanced countries—for the attainment by women of social equality. But we ought not forget that the

---

In Volume I of *The Psychology of Women* (1944) I presented an extensive study of the adolescence of girls. In this monograph, the adolescence of girls is viewed in the light of contemporary events.

fights, and the victories, were not always restricted solely to the question of "equal rights."

Biological realities, for example, created specific needs on the part of women, connected with the particular tasks of women as females. In addition to equal opportunities for social functioning and equal compensation for socially productive activity, there was also the goal of *special rights for women,* insofar as they were engaged "in the service of the species." It was a difficult and often long and strenuous task to mobilize effective consideration for the problems faced by women—particularly working-class women—with regard to pregnancy, delivery, the lactation period, and the neonate and infancy periods of their children's lives. That struggle was to a high degree successful, especially in the achievements of organized labor.

The fight for "women's rights" is now no longer directed toward laws and social organizations. It turns rather to cultural and individual values and rests in the hands of the young women themselves—in their ability to perform within the framework of the opportunities and guarantees that have already been won for women in the social sphere, to achieve what they can achieve there without far-reaching sacrifices in regard to their *fundamental rights of motherhood.*

GROUP FORMATION IN ADOLESCENT GIRLS

This modest survey of the group activities of adolescent girls, as well as of the individual roots of these activities, deals with the problems that appear en route to the goal (or goals) of their mature womanhood. To a great extent, as far as the girls are concerned, the "adolescent revolution" is most overtly and forcefully expressed as a fight for "equal rights to sexual freedom," the latter having been until now definitely restricted for girls, as compared with what had been attained by the boys.

Generally, the group formations of adolescent girls, like those of the boys, have been at one and the same time expressions of revolutionary protest, and expressions of both progressive and regressive forces that come to the fore in the process of maturation. We shall see what a large part is played in the formation and orientation of the group activities of the girls by their passive identification with the boys, which only occasionally reflects their underlying and inherent penis envy.

Group formations in which a definite ideology transcends the personal revolution serve to unite the girls with the boys in the name of this ideology, and thus do not reflect, anywhere nearly as strongly as do other adolescent groups, the force of individual motivations. Unfortunately, the wider setting of social progress toward sexual freedom for girls is not without its repercussions, and the sometimes tragic consequences of this freedom are found even there, although less characteristically than in other adolescent groups.

In this final chapter of the monograph, more than in our observations on the boys, we shall see how certain *infantile* elements in development have remained apart from the general process of the girls' maturation, to create personalities of the sort that we all too frequently encounter these days in the world of intellectually very mature women.

After these brief introductory remarks, let us return to our central problem of the group formations of contemporary adolescents. These are definitely mixed, as far as the sex of its participants is concerned. Nevertheless, there are certain manifestations, even within the conformity of the group, that make it advisable to take a separate look at the girls, starting with their first appearance in public life, as a group, or rather mass—that noisy Beatle-addicted conglomeration of girls in their early adolescence (between thirteen and fifteen), with which we have become all too familiar. We are confronted indirectly here with developmental problems in girls of this age. These crucial years of personality formation cannot be presented *in extenso* here. As a frame of reference, one may apply direct and numerous observations of individual cases of the adolescence of girls, as described in the psychoanalytic literature (H. Deutsch, 1944, pp. 25-184; Blos, 1962).

One major characteristic of this group is a certain compromise between a still persistent latent homosexuality and an awakening striving toward heterosexuality. This compromise is very often expressed in a typical adolescent triangle: one boy and two girls, both of whom are involved in a romantic, exaggerated love for the boy. The "Beatles" situation is in fact a reproduction of this triangle; mass involvement is a psychologically identical situation, only with a different numerical distribution: thousands of girls in place of two, and one boy splintered into the four figures of the musical group. It is an acting out of developmental tensions in a largely unorganized group of individuals who are identical with regard to their emotional situation.

Externalization of a heavy-laden fantasy life; control of tensions and longing by the critical attention of the public; exhibition of emotions, without guilt feelings ("we're all doing it"); wild outbursts of gross sexual excitement; jealous competition with other girls, in which there is no victor; and, above all, gratification of a still existent erotic bond with one's own girlfriends—all these constitute the psychological background for the first early adolescent group formation.[1] Boys in early adolescence were, of course, also involved with the Beatles—but in a different way. Jealousy and a tendency to identification with the Beatles were very evident; they even influenced certain behavioral attitudes on the part of many boys (musical groups à la Beatles, imitation of their appearance, etc.).

Although the Beatle craze was an organization of "girls only," it led directly to later group formations of a mixed character: boys and girls. Let me briefly repeat here an observation I made earlier with regard to group formations in

[1] Miss Heidi Wermer, a fifteen-year-old girl, who had just recently outgrown her own Beatle period, was very helpful in my efforts to understand the Beatle craze.

adolescence: whether they are primitive or sophisticated in character, irrational or highly motivated in their goals, *all* adolescent groups have two main goals: as a vehicle for rebellion, and as a sort of counterphobic refuge from that anxiety in which "Alone, *I* am lost; together, *we* are strong."

In Chapter 3, I described group formations that, while they were not yet organized, were nevertheless already marked by definite and characteristic traits and attitudes. In discussing this sort of group, I emphasized the core of rebellion, the change of external habitus, and, above all, the absolute conformity of the group members. In addition, various more individual attitudes revealed themselves as expressions of a tendency toward regressive acting out.

For the most part, among the groups of early adolescence, we meet with young girls as active participants. What was the specific behavior of these girls? They identified with the boys, thereby adding to the conformist character of the group. They dressed like the boys, for example, in that way emphasizing even more strongly the factor of dirtiness as a sort of triumph against the mother (some mothers have told me that the girls dressed neatly enough at home, but that, even after they had taken their usual morning bath, they would then dirty their hair and clothes, before joining the group on the street). They tried to participate in all the rebellious activities of the boys—and they succeeded in doing so.

Does this mean that the girls wanted to be boys? Only in individual cases did this identification with boys express masculinity; or, in very active girls, it may have been a continuation of the previous "push toward activity." What the girls intended, above all, was to get away from the exclusiveness of "only girls"; as the Beatle enthusiasm faded, their still very labile heterosexuality, which had been progressing with maturation, became a source of increased anxiety for them. Certain peculiarities in their behavior were definitely in the service of their defenses. The interplay feminine-masculine, with them as with the boys, took the form of a masquerade.

One could hardly avoid drawing analogies with the boys who were participants in the same group activities. In both sexes, bisexual traits dominated their external appearance. Whether the biological events of adolescence reinforced the constitutional bisexual Anlage is difficult to say; I can refer only to those psychological forces that determine the adolescents' attitudes.

Let us not forget that the resolution of the oedipus complex in adolescence, paradoxically, has the effect of mobilizing various regressive elements. The identification with the parents is not unilinear, but goes through a succession of different periods, in which vacillation between father and mother is very characteristic. This may be responsible, to a great extent, for the bisexual behavior that is shown by both sexes during adolescence. The overwhelming anxiety of boys during this period is provoked by the invasion of biological maturity. There is no analogy for this in girls. Their sexual progress is not as acute, and it is only by and by that biological changes—above all, the advent of menstruation—exert an influence on their psychological reactions. Their budding femininity is still very much anchored in fantasies, one of which is revealed impressively in their makeup, which to my mind is associated with "Lorelei" and her straight, long golden hair, typical of this prototype of female seductiveness in German folklore.[2] "Lorelei" is the German version of the

2 *Encyclopedia Britannica,* Volume 14:
LORELEI a rock in the Rhine near St. Goar, which gives a remarkable echo (O.H.G. *Lur,* connected with modern Ger. *lauern,* "to lurk" "be on the watch for," and equivalent to elf, and *lai,* "a rock"). In the most common form of the story, the Lorelei is a maiden who threw herself into the Rhine in despair over a faithless lover, and became a siren whose voice lured fishermen to destruction. The tale is closely connected with the myth of Holda, queen of the elves. The man who sees her loses sight of reason; he who listens is condemned to wander with her forever. In the 19th century, the legend was material for a number of songs, dramatic sketches, etc. The favorite poem with composers was Heine's, beginning *Ich weiss nicht was soll es bedeuten.*

siren who often appears in ancient mythology, always in the role of seducing and destroying the unfortunate lover, but in most cases also herself. The power of this seductiveness is expressed in the episode of Odysseus' journey in which he lashes himself to the mast of the ship in order to resist the danger of seduction. Long straight golden hair has been, during recent years, almost a compulsion, a must with our adolescent girls. The hair has to hang loose over the shoulders and to be absolutely straight (some girls even press their hair with an iron).

The lower body of these young girls, however, is in contrast to their golden-haired femininity. It is clad in dilapidated jeans, with an emphasis on negligence and masculinity. Continuing my analogy with the sirens, I am inclined to see in this part of the masquerade a kind of identity with the fishtail of the sirens. It is impressive how adolescents seem to mobilize fantasies that are also found in legends. I regard a young girl's demonstration that she is a boy as a classical defense against the feminine seductiveness of the symbolic blond hair: under the pressure of anxiety, every expression of sexuality has to be defensively counteracted. The flight into masculinity provides a refuge, not only from the dangers of sexuality in general, but specifically from the masochistic element in femininity. One can thus say that the girls' bisexual appearance is at one and the same time an expression of their feminine fantasies and an identification with the boys in *their* rebellion, as well as the use of that identification as defense!

SEXUAL FREEDOM

It may seem paradoxical to say that, at the very time when they employ these defenses, boys and girls in these rebellious groups are involved in intensive "sexual fooling." What is disquieting for the observer is that the usual sentimental romantic love is cast away, by this generation of youth, as though it were no more than an old shoe. The guilt feeling in this regard also uses the "we" as protection: the forbidden is not performed as an individual action, but is elevated instead to a "change of society," a "new generation," a "better world." We have to try to understand these adolescents and their "new form of life," which implies, according to them, a truth that is rooted in human nature, and thus free from the hypocrisy that marked the life of their predecessors.

These new trends place special emphasis on sexual freedom for girls: the new morality not only assumes the right of girls to sexual freedom, it makes the utilization of that freedom a kind of obligation. When one keeps in mind, however, the well-known fact that the ego ideal of the girl is built to a great extent on the mother—the ideal mother, not the sexually devalued one—one realizes how deeply rooted is the girls' basic attitude toward chastity. The transgression of sexual boundaries, among these young girls, is therefore seldom real sexual freedom; their guilt reactions are indeed very strong.

With regard to the further development of the ego ideal, this so-called social progress is thus not a constructive force; one could even say that the ego ideal is shattered by it. The adolescent girl's devaluation of the mother is built on regressive forces, in which the psychological situations of the past once again come into action. One of those past situations was the discovery that the mother's "chastity" was not real. Another had to do with the phallic phase, in which mother too was found to be castrated. Whenever a rebellious youth looks for reasons for contempt for his parents, he winds up rationalizing his contempt in terms of "sexual perfidy," etc. In fact, this devaluation is rooted regressively in the period of the usual devaluation of overidealized parents.

I consider those girls who are involved prematurely in "free love" as not the victors but the victims of the rebellious adolescent society. A great number of them are still involved in their earlier relationships with girlfriends. They "fool around," as the saying goes, with boys—but it is still with a side glance at the girls, and their heterosexual activity actually shows very little inner participation. One sees them dancing with violent contortions of their bodies, sexual-looking exhibitions and grossly erotic gestures; yet one cannot help observing the lack of any object relationship in their performance. The partner is, in effect, no more than a point of orientation.

They may even be sexually involved with boys, and yet these involvements too do not have very much to do with their progress toward femininity. Their activity usually shows a marked increase of oral gratification: they smoke, drink, use drugs indiscriminately; in individual variations, their increased aggressiveness may involve them in acts of stupid destructiveness. Both their social milieu and their individual differences play a decisive role during the course of these activities.

The so-called sexual revolution is built on the assumption of the young rebels that complete sexual freedom and unlimited sexual activity are the signs of progress and of new values. The very young boy of these early adolescent groups, who is paralyzed by anxiety, appears on the social scene, disregarding his long hair in the role of the "He-man," and seeking to overcompensate his anxiety by way of uninhibited sexual activity. The biological urge in boys often makes them energetic and insistent, and their rebellious phraseology helps to overcome the young girls' inhibitions.

In observing this new sexual freedom, however, we "older folks" do not show the reactions expected by the young people. We do not conceive of it as a confrontation of social stagnation with social progress, as it is both proclaimed and intended by the young people: "out of the bondage of social prejudices!" "real freedom of sex!" etc. We rather ask ourselves: is this *really* a "new" form of life, something that is progressive and implies—as we repeatedly hear —"a *truth* rooted in human nature, free from the hypocrisy of our predecessors"? No one who observes carefully can fail to see that this "new freedom," for all that it promises happiness, seems not to keep its promise.

I myself have never seen more unhappy-looking boys and girls. Their triumph is not one of victorious youth, but of hate-filled, resentful young people who, for all that they may have aspirations toward achievement and progress, evidently suffer from emotional deprivation and a kind of deadening, as a result, of their so-called free and unlimited sexual excitement. Cases of addiction—especially of addiction to LSD, which I have had the opportunity to observe—have shown me clearly that, in those very young people, the all-too-often repeated and all-too-easily attainable sexual gratification does not bring any real emotional fulfillment. The spasmodic search for methods by which to increase the pleasure of the sexual experience indicates unmistakably that the sexual freedom of our adolescents does not provide the ecstatic element that is inherent—or should be—in one of the most gratifying of human experiences.

That experience does not need any intensification, if it is not hampered by anxiety or by the lack of erotic feelings. When one observes these sexually active young people, one sometimes has the impression that for them sexual activity is not a way to satisfy their biological needs, but is "glorified" instead into a way to spite their parents and their parents' society, as well as to prove their own superiority over the "miserable, corrupt" world of their predecessors. The inadequacy for them of the sexual experience as such is expressed not only in their need of drugs, but also in the increasing interest they show in sexual perversions.

I think that the *lack* of any deeper emotional participation —of longing and wishing, of pain and joy, of hope and despair—along with this glorification of the coveted object, constitutes a psychological disaster. In addition, the inner work of the transformation of narcissism into object relationship does not take place; the sublimation of instinctual drives to tenderness is to a great extent simply absent. The attempt to debase the emotional values of *homo sapiens,* by replacing them with the more primitive ways of direct, biologically preformed functions, is not actually gratifying for young souls. And since the need for values is, in this generation too, if not inherited from, at least developed by, the educational influences of the environment, the deficiency of emotional values has to be compensated for. This is done by phraseology about "progress," "new generation," and by stereotyped accusations against society, etc. There is no question, however, that a too early involvement in sexual gratification interferes with the development of real, tender feelings of love and enchantment.

In girls, the problem is more complicated and the sexual freedom is accordingly even more revolutionary. For the girl, it is a part of her general emancipation, the demand for the equality of sexes. It is at the same time a break in the fortress within which the ego ideal of the girl was built—in this generation no less than in previous ones.

The restitution of the capacity to love, through correction of the acquired tendency to separate love from purely sexual gratification, may take place later, and in girls more easily than in boys. Sometimes a favorable identification, a successful intervention from the outside, an unexpected old-fashioned case of falling in love—these may bring a kind of recovery with regard to the deficient elements of the girl's maturation process. And always there is the rich wealth of potential motherhood in every female being, which may supply the impoverished ego with reinforcements—provided that it is not too late for it to do so, and that the process of maturation is not petrified.

In observing the rebellious activities of adolescents—especially of girls, in their fight for sexual freedom—one cannot ignore the victims of their hostilely critical attacks: the parents. In previous generations, the parents were "in the other camp." They sought to *counteract* the efforts of their adolescent children to free themselves from their dependency by actively loosening their ties to home. In the contemporary struggle between generations, however, the problems are more complicated. Many parents—especially mothers—have a strong desire to be "modern" too: they show "tolerance," abdicate their parental authority, and even go so far as to collaborate in the rebellious activities of their children. The young people are, in effect, "let loose to freedom" with their parents' collaboration. They do not really want this, of course, because they would prefer—and actually need—to fight for it. While their inner efforts toward freedom are mobilized, their ego has not yet reached the degree of maturity that would enable it to provide them with the capacity to struggle, to build defenses, by and by to replace the lost objects of childhood with new objects.

The parents, not having been successful in their own adolescent revolution, sometimes hope to achieve a kind of delayed victory through identification with their children. In all strata of society, one can observe this uncertainty of parents as to what to do. They are hesitant, apparently unaware that the adolescents—with all their aggressive protests, with all their proclamations of independence and of the new values that they are trying to bring to society—are actually very unsure of themselves and often seeking desperately for guidance. Unfortunately, in many instances, these adolescents find approval in just those places where they would wish to find challengeable restrictions. Especially in problems of sexuality, the parents—more often, the mothers—accept the sexual rebellion of their children, not as a result of their own inner conviction but out of embarrassment and uncertainty as to what is right and what is wrong in sexual behavior, or as to what is only confusion and rebelliousness among the younger generation and what has it in the seeds of real progress.

In her wish to be modern, to "understand" her daughter, to participate in social progress by consent, the mother often pushes and directs her daughter toward activities such as she

herself never dared to engage in. In her own narcissistic expectations, now transferred onto her daughter, she cannot
tolerate the possibility that the latter may have fewer boys
interested in her than in other girls; she feels deprived herself if the daughter is not dating enough. Last but not least,
the modern mother is quite alarmed by the problem of
homosexuality and, out of fear of its widening scope, sup-
ports aggressively her son's precocious heterosexuality. She
also views with suspicion her daughter's friendships with
girls and even prefers for her the dangers of heterosexuality.

The mother's identification with her daughter often takes
a grotesque form. She herself gives up her own more conservative way of living and emerges instead as a participant
in adolescent conformity. It is not very unusual to meet with
two adolescent females—each with her own long blond hair,
dungarees and all the "modern girl's" paraphernalia—only
to discover that this is mother and daughter, the former with
feelings of triumph against her own mother, the latter probably deeply hurt and furious with hers.[3]

In this parental attitude of compliance, the adolescent
finds evidence of the fact that the adult world indeed lacks
solidity and clarity in matters of sexual behavior, and that its
values with regard to sexuality are truly shaky and cloudy.
The inability of the older generation to exert authority is
then interpreted by the rebellious youth as a new sign of that
generation's demoralization and lack of real values.

Unfortunately, the confusions and the impulsive actions

[3] A wonderful example of such a contemporary performance is shown in
the work as well as the personal appearance of a French sculptress. Her sculp-
tures often seem to have the same theme: a gigantic female figure, which is
composed of round masses that suggest the lower and upper parts of her
body. On top is a tiny little head, which no doubt indicates the woman's
lack of brain. In photographs of this sculpture, one recognizes the artist herself: a prototype of the contemporary adolescent with loose-hanging hair. She
is the mother of an adolescent girl who probably looks like her mother—in
an identity that was not created by the girl herself, but *in reverse* by her
mother, who is a generation older, and *still in protest* against her own
"brainless" mother.

of early adolescence, along with its rebellious attitude toward restrictions, have often brought these girls into tragic entanglements before their maturational process has been able to endow them with adequate defenses. True enough, they become mothers very early—in the physiological meaning of motherhood. But alas! menstruation did not make them women earlier, and giving birth to a child does not now make them mothers.

ILLEGITIMATE MOTHERHOOD

The social and personal catastrophe of illegitimate motherhood on the part of very young girls is rapidly on the increase. Statistics that were valid yesterday may already be antiquated today. Not long ago, these girls were called "dropouts"; that category also included some girls, however, whose interruption of their education was for less ominous reasons. A number of intelligent girls, who are promising seniors in high school, drop out because they are afraid of not being accepted in college. They prefer giving up to being rejected! It is thus still possible to restore them to their school status after this interruption. (Here is a good example, indeed, of narcissistic vulnerability!)

Reports on the other dropouts, however, are more sinister. There have been various such reports, of which one from Connecticut was the first to cause alarm in the country. According to this estimate, one out of every seven girls between thirteen and eighteen in Connecticut was the victim of an unwed pregnancy. Later came the report from a Springfield, Mass. high school: "Fifty-two girls dropped out last year because they were pregnant." Information that has since been made public indicates that high school pregnancies are on the increase: their numbers are no longer to be reckoned in tens, but in hundreds and even thousands.

While these statistics refer only to pregnancies, the number of schoolgirls who have already given birth to a child is quite startling. Many of these girls come from conservative, dignified families; as a result, they are often not included in these reports because they left school for "reasons of health."

School authorities do not any longer meet the situation on an individual basis, but as a mass problem. Nor can their intervention any longer be limited to problems of prevention, but has to include plans for the care and further education of these pregnant young girls.

This motherhood has, in most cases, a definite character from its beginning: the father is usually a young boy, who has been involved in mutual masturbatory activities with the girl; after a while, this has led to intercourse. It is difficult to say here who is actually the seducer and who the seduced. No precautions are taken—which has absolutely nothing to do with lack of sexual information. That is a misunderstanding, on which future preventive acts of authorities cannot afford to be based. Sexual instructions are no remedy, and neither are pills: the pregnancy of these girls is *compulsive,* and compulsive acts resist *any* interference with them.

A schoolgirl's pregnancy is kept secret by her as long as is possible; any attempt to terminate it is rejected. Sometimes knowledge of a girl's impending motherhood is confined to the girl's friend (or friends), and even there more as a sensation than as a tragedy. Peculiarly enough, there seems to be a trend toward a concentration of cases of pregnancy in one and the same school (for example, Springfield). This does not indicate the presence of a "wolf" in the school, but rather a certain atmosphere among the girls, along with their need to share the adventurous sensation. They may be the same girls who, in their even earlier development (eleven to twelve), played at motherhood together, by putting pillows under their skirts and exchanging their secret "knowledge" of anatomy and physiology.

Illegitimate pregnancies are nothing new, and even pregnancies among very young girls have long been known to social agencies. The responsibility often lay with the social environment in which certain emotional conflicts arose and were then acted out. The baby was usually an "oedipal" child, born under the pressure of family events. Among certain groups of the population, however, illegitimacy is today an everyday event. In Negro families, for example, the child is generally brought to the mother of the girl, who takes loving care of it; the problems thereafter are mainly of a financial nature. In some other countries—for example, in the West Indies—illegitimate babies also exist in great numbers: they are brought immediately after birth to the grandmother; the baby's father often does not play any role at all, beyond that of impregnation. All these children are culturally assigned, as it were, to be born by the daughter, and "owned" and educated by the grandmother. In our culture, by contrast, the father is an important part of the situation and the grandmother's role is reduced to that of baby sitting.

My further investigations into individual cases of these young schoolgirls' experiences with motherhood indicate that we are dealing here with a specific phenomenon. What could previously be seen only in rare individual cases has now become a mass event. But the psychological process that was observed in individuals can also have meaning for the social problem. If we call the illegitimate pregnancies "precocious," we can easily see in them the direct consequences of activities that express the new sexual freedom. This is certainly responsible to a great extent for the weakening of the young girl's usual inhibitions. If further observations do not contradict my conception, one can lay the blame for these pregnancies of very immature girls, it seems to me, on a certain disposition that is revived by the regressive processes in adolescence and, above all, by the maturational demand to break off the earlier attachment to mother.

That disposition is rooted in the preoedipal, oral stage of development—which makes this attachment the most powerful force in the psychological functioning of these girls. The longing for mother, the desperate feeling of loneliness upon being separated from her, calls for revival of the mother-child union. This may sometimes be achieved in an intimate relationship with an older woman, in which the situation is realized in direct sexual activities (H. Deutsch, 1932). It may be limited to fantasies, which are often converted into somatic reactions. In our cases, the fantasy is reinforced by sexually exciting games with boys, and it is only reality that changes the childish game into a serious catastrophe. Nevertheless, the role of the partner in this intimate situation is actually that of the mother, and the boy's embrace is a substitute for the longed-for reunion with her. The sexual sequel, the impregnation, brings with it a continuation of the fantasy: mother-child unity is achieved through pregnancy and in relationship to the unborn child, whose role usually ends with its real existence after delivery.

The question then arises: why does this happen in our times and as a mass phenomenon? The answer is not settled by reference to the "sexual freedom" of contemporary adolescents; it also lies in social developments within our conventional society. Perhaps, under the rebellious pressure of the young generation, society, in its adoption of "progressive" attitudes toward sexuality and in its offers of understanding and help, seems to extend a kind of permission to do what is generally thought of as "not permitted." This may appear, to the still somewhat childish minds of these young girls, to mean an advice—even, perhaps, a push—to be free and to use this freedom in the service of their fantasies. I do not believe that enlightenment and even pills can prevent the catastrophic events that do occur. As I have noted above, compulsions are stronger than any realistic approach. This does not mean, of course, that all girls are exposed to the effects of the "new" sexual freedom, but it is becoming clear that far more of them are so exposed than we had known about earlier.

It may appear that I have made society solely responsible for motherhood in early adolescence. The fact is that I consider society to be only an *agent provocateur* for certain deep-rooted forces at work during this *specific* phase of adolescence and among *specific* individuals who are genetically disposed to such reactions. I am not unaware, of course, that society is assigned by these adolescent girls a certain role that fits into the whole scheme of their individual functioning.

Peter Blos (1962), speaking about the delinquency of boys during puberty, refers to the arrest of emotional development at the preoedipal level, in which the mother is the ominous castrating power, the witch of folklore. The boys' passivity and castration anxiety is centered on this preoedipal mother relationship. (There is also a positive aspect of this relationship, however, which I have discussed in Chapter 2.)

Blos (1962) says that in female delinquency, which, broadly speaking, represents sexual acting-out behavior, the fixation on the preoedipal mother plays a most decisive role. "The pseudoheterosexuality of the delinquent girl serves as a defense against the regressive pull to the preoedipal mother" (p. 236). Blos attempts to bring girls and boys into analogy with each other via their delinquent traits. According to him, it is the preoedipal fixation in both that is responsible for their abnormal actions.

In boys, however, the fixation is at the phallic period, whereas the girls' adolescent process of maturation is more hampered by arrest at the oral stage and by the fact that the relationship to mother is anchored at that period. Generally speaking, I find that the *oral* dependency on mother plays a greater role in the development of girls than in that of boys. It is responsible for various forms of pathology (hysteria and paranoia) (R. M. Brunswick, 1940), for a definite kind of homosexuality (H. Deutsch, 1932), and above all for a personality structure that I shall call *infantilism*.

Blos (1962) reports the case history of a thirteen-year-old delinquent girl, which runs: Nancy was obsessed by the wish for a baby—all her sexual fantasies pointed to the mother-baby theme and basically to an overwhelming oral greed. "She had a dream in which she had sexual relations with teenage boys; in the dream she had 365 babies, one a day for a year from one boy, whom she shot after this was accomplished" (p. 236). Nancy seems to fit my image of juvenile mothers.

INFANTILISM

I would like to give a brief description of infantilism as an entity. In reviewing the maturational process of adolescence, we pay attention to all the facets of adolescent personality, in boys and girls alike: their libidinal situation, involved as it is in struggle with the oedipus complex in all its ramifications; their bisexual problems; their narcissism; their ego ideal and superego; their identity crises; and their victorious adaptation to the events in the role of a man or a woman.

These analogies end, however, at the moment when we include the girls' development toward motherhood. It is one of those developmental paradoxa that makes me bring in the problem of infantilism as the factor most responsible for the young girl's "precocious" motherhood!

The infantile personality is characterized by the narcissistic need to be loved. Intolerance of frustration is marked, yet every gratification itself bears the seed of frustration. The role of the *pleasure principle* is tyrannical; an ever-present impatience to reach a pleasure goal creates a kind of spasmodic activity (acting out) in an otherwise generally passive personality. Their sexual fantasies are filled with wild and often quite romantic contests; the excitation is predominantly anal; clitoris masturbation is usually limited to sexual play with a partner (girl or boy).

These girls respond very quickly to seduction, not because of the intensity of their sexual appetite but because of pleasure hunger. While they are actually craving, they remain frigid during the sexual act. They desperately want togetherness, yet they always remain alone. Even though the feeling of loneliness is very strong, no intimacy is able to gratify this painful sensation, because what it expresses is the longing

of the child in his oral relationship to mother. Their superego and ego ideal are very feebly internalized. They may
obey orders, even act upon them; they may fear punishment
and make efforts to avoid it. Yet all their limiting as well as
their permissive forces come less from within than from the
external world.

The level of functioning will depend upon the social environment. They seldom show apathy, but often suffer depressive moods (of short duration). This usually occurs when
the supply of pleasure and of narcissistic gratification is not
available. They often have artistic talents: they make fine
"nothingnesses," such as colorful costume jewelry, naïve
paintings, attractive little shawls, etc. The number of shops
with this kind of applied art is increasing with the number
of infantile adolescent girls.

Since this is a developmental stage that is apparently arrested in infancy and then revived regressively in early adolescence, one is compelled to ask: what was the cause of the
fixation, and what are its reviving forces?

During the last year, I observed in consultation a fifteen-
year-old girl whose pregnancy never became a school problem because, once it was discovered in time by the mother,
it came under the latter's control. The mother told me that
the girl had fought for the continuation of her pregnancy
and that one could do nothing without the girl's agreement.
At the time when the girl was still a little child (two to three
years old), the mother had been in psychoanalytic treatment
with me. At that time, she was already overactive in her relationship to the child. It had been impossible for her either
to tolerate or to expose the child to any frustration; every
frustrating situation for the child was immediately counteracted by the mother with some form of gratification, thereby
reinforcing in the child the dominance of the pleasure principle.

I have analyzed quite a number of mothers who exhibited
a similar intolerance toward any sign of unpleasure in their

small children. They themselves were able to take a great amount of personal suffering with a somewhat masochistic attitude, but they were intolerant toward any discomfort shown by their children. One of them nursed her child for a very long time, because she was not able to inflict upon it the "trauma of weaning." According to our experience, nothing is so predisposing to traumatic reactions as the successful avoidance of what are usually unavoidable traumas. In our case, whenever such avoidance seemed impossible, the mother was there with her compensatory actions—an attitude that develops in the child a burning need for passively received compensations and thereby interferes with the development of active defense mechanisms.

The effect of the mother's attitude is the development in the child of a low threshold of tolerance toward unpleasure, which in turn provokes a certain kind of activity in pursuit of pleasure. This is what is responsible, it seems to me, for many of the so-called "crazy doings" in early adolescence (acting out). Along with this acting out, there is a characteristic tendency to passivity and a waiting for supply. This all too gratifying bond with the mother has to be severed in adolescence by the demands of maturation. The actual separation from mother that is forced upon the girl by psychological developments, or by the demands of reality, is for her a signal to create new bonds. These are expected to replace the mother and yet to provide the "child" with the same kind of gratification as she received from the mother during her earlier years.

I think that the majority of the very young mothers fit into this concept of infantilism. Their compulsive pregnancy is not the expression of a woman's wish and need to be a mother. They are usually deserted by the child's sire, in the main because no real emotional bond has developed between him and the girl. Whatever tragic complications may develop in the girl's reality, the compulsion may persist, and the girl may repeat the experience. A seventeen-year-old girl,

who was already three times a mother, is not a unique
example.

These infantile girls have little or no relationship to their
child; they sever their mother-child bond almost immediately
after the birth and leave the further fate of the newborn in
the hands of society. Their activity is not an acting out of an
oedipal wish for a child, nor is their motherhood on the level
of "assistant mother"—that is, of an adolescent girl who is
not yet ready for motherhood and gratifies her feminine wish
as a mother's helper (see H. Deutsch, 1945). In the infantile
girl, the lack of internalization and of reliable ego ideal and
superego formation brings her relationship to reality under
the guidance of external powers: it is only as long as parental
authority was in a position to guide her life that it was under
control.

In the more mature adolescents, transgressions are among
their typical attempts to throw off the guidance of authority.
Among girls, the aggressive ambivalence toward the mother
often expresses itself in antisocial behavior—especially of a
sexual character. For our infantile girls, however, the new
trend of sexual freedom was, paradoxically, the voice of *external authority,* which joined with the "anti-mother" forces
within, in the permission of gratifications that had previously
been forbidden by the mother. There will doubtless be a
new, more energetic attempt on the part of school authorities
to decrease the evil by information, sexual enlightenment,
etc. For these girls, however, such efforts may constitute no
more than a new incitement to compulsive actions!

I have mentioned the importance of the failure in the
development of these girls in regard to various parts of their
so-called "structural functioning"—that is, in their ability
to form a consolidated ego ideal as well as a superego. This
weakness of ego organization deprives these girls of an important element of self-regulatory control and of the basis for
sexual inhibition.

The taboo of virginity crumbles during the early period

of development toward femininity; the oral urgency for gratification then creates an ominous situation. I was impressed
by the mothers' contribution to the persistence of the pleasure principle, as well as to the deficiency in the girls' identification with the mother on a higher level. The fact that the
influence of cultural development then proved decisive in
these cases was due to the *inner* situation: the impact upon
the behavior of *external* factors was no more than the work
of an *agent provocateur*.

One may even speculate that society, with its more permissive attitude, took on the role of the father who allies
himself with the little girl against the formerly permissive
but now forbidding mother. If we disregard the whole attitude during pregnancy and after the birth of the child, which
is filled with hostility against the mother, the girl's guilt reactions toward her are very evident.

I am pessimistic, however, with regard to the possibility
that pregnancy itself may have any positive value for development toward real motherhood. These unfortunate girls often
tend to repeat their pregnancy, very soon after the first has
been completed. The traumatic event has brought no resolution, but rather an even further inhibiting effect on their
development toward real motherhood.

Since infantilism will be of further interest to us in its
meaning for later adolescence, I would like to give an even
clearer description of it.

Contact with reality is fully preserved, and the process of
adaptation is not badly impaired. There is no real breakdown
of ego integration or of ego identity. While object relationships have a sticky, clinging character, they are without either
constancy or reciprocity. The orality shows an autoerotic
character and demands childish forms of gratification (chew-
ing candies constantly; a craving for sweets). The tendency
is to act out fantasies, when that acting out can be a source
of immediate pleasure.

When we speak about oral fixation, we assume that dis-

positional elements must have been reinforced by experiences
during that period of childhood. I have no direct observations on children, and my analytic experience with this form
of primitive infantilism is very limited. But I do know some
of the mothers and I regard them as a very rewarding source
of information. Sometimes the childhood history of these
children reveals jealousy of a younger sibling, not of a phallic
but an oral character; sometimes it is the separation from
mother that constitutes the traumatic and fixating element.
But I find that the formation of the infantile personality as
a definite psychic structure is usually the product of the
mother's personality and of her relationship to the child.
Specifically, I have observed that the government of the
child's ego by the pleasure principle has been unmistakably
due to the mother's influence upon the child. My own experience, which is confirmed by many of my professional
friends, seems to indicate that, in psychoanalytic practice, we
are increasingly being confronted with infantile personalities.

To return to the mothers of infantile daughters, we must
add another type of mother, whose personality gives rise
correspondingly to another type of infantilism in their
daughters. These are women who show a very paradoxical
attitude toward their children: on the one hand, they have
great difficulty letting their children grow up and become
actively and really independent; on the other hand, it is these
same mothers who, because of their own narcissism, actually
push the children toward precocious development, and this
pushing may lead to traumatic reactions of a lasting nature.

I want to demonstrate the effect of this process in the case
of a girl in her later adolescence whom I recently analyzed.
Her personality was quite different from that of the girls
described above; nevertheless, her development was based
on fundamentally similar psychological conditions.

Betty is a twenty-year-old college girl, who comes from a
very intellectual family. The mother is extremely ambitious,
but thwarted by the situation of her generation: women

could not, at that time, so easily gratify their ambitions; in their society, there was still a deep-rooted conviction that mother has to "stay at home." As a result, the mother lavished gratifications on her small child; and, when Betty was three years old, the mother decided that the child was "unusual"—whereupon she devoted herself to the education of the girl, who had really shown signs of great intelligence. Having decided at that time that the girl would be a great poet, she memorized poetry together with her for hours. In this narcissistic union with the mother, the girl collaborated eagerly.

Later came the shared fantasy that the child would become a great painter; every picture made by the girl was now regarded as a real work of art, shown to authorities, etc. When Betty was eight years old, she was already reading books written for adults. Since she was able to memorize a good deal, she was regarded by the mother and her friends as a future celebrity. Even in childhood, she was already absolutely intolerant of any unpleasure, and there was a marked orality in her direct cravings, her food allergies, etc. One can well imagine how this pushing toward maturity in one direction must have been linked with deprivation in another: "a big girl like you. . . ."

When I met the patient, she was still able to carry through a good intellectual performance, as an honor student in her junior year, but her personality was exactly at the level of the little girl: intolerant of frustration. She would suddenly leave her class when the idea came to her that she wanted to buy a dress she had seen in a window; or she would run out to buy something exotic to eat. She could never resist an erotic temptation—if it promised to give her excitement and narcissistic gratification.

From time to time—usually under some provocation of a frustrating character—she went into retirement, to passivity with a tendency to depressions. These were always connected with an increased but not yet gratified need of pleasure and

of narcissistic gratification. As long as she was able to maintain the pleasure equilibrium, she remained normal. But
when the reality was too difficult for her to handle, when
the normal obstacles encountered in life—such as competition, criticism from her superiors, etc.—were too difficult for
her to master, she had strong frustration reactions: rage, depressions, masochistic acting out. The most characteristic aspect of these reactions was that she was not able to conquer
her passivity in a normal way. At such times, the supply had
to come "from the mother"—that is, from mother substitutes
in the external world.

Betty was constantly preoccupied with her appearance:
how she looked and how she was impressing others. Her con-
cern for status was very strongly connected with her academic
ambition, but not exclusively: *good standing in the eyes of
others* was extended to everything; it was the center of her
interest in life. I quote: "I look for pleasure, and avoid everything that interferes with it; I buy dresses, go dancing and do
exercises in order to keep myself whole, to prevent myself
from falling apart." She also worried about her overeating.
It was extremely important to her to be slender, and she
needed a good deal of energy in order to establish an equilibrium between her narcissistic wishes for a good figure, on
the one hand, and the pleasure principle (eating) on the
other.

In my interviews with college girls, I was astonished by the
frequency with which, even if in individual variations, Betty-
like personalities made their appearance. Their work was also
for a "good showing"; it was performed with skill and intelligence, but apparently primarily for their own glory and
narcissistic gratification. Girls like these have smooth sailing
into adolescence. They enjoy their brilliance in school, and
they are readily accepted into the prestige colleges (according
to the mother's plans, which were made when the daughters
were only three years old). They do very well, and are respected for it by their colleagues; but they are not often

loved. Quite the contrary; they are usually disliked because of the competitiveness, their demonstrations of narcissism, and their aggressive reactions to provocations of unpleasure. While they may grow in certain particular areas, they do not really mature, and they do not show any evidence of stronger oedipal involvements. They may be "daddy's little girls," with an excellent mutual understanding between them, and sometimes even an alliance against mother; but that is all.

I do not known why these girls, who are anchored in pre-oedipal situations, do not revive and solve their shrunken oedipal problems during the process of maturation; after all, they did have fathers! Perhaps their fragile development had no support during their adolescence in external conditions. Perhaps there was no paternal figure whose personality would fit adequately the girl's conception of "father." I have often heard college girls complaining that their teachers are either "dried-out scholars," or else behave like young boys who are looking for adventure. I was not able to convince them that this was simply their own image of these men. They had, unfortunately, examples to prove their point: men in high positions, who were involved in erotic interplay with younger females, tended to reject the fatherly role and instead take the attitude of adolescent boys. The love of a young girl fits *their* wish for rejuvenation; but usually this clash of expectations ends in separation. The girl may then turn to her contemporary young man and try to go along with his illusion that the beard he is wearing makes him an "older" man. This observation does not deny the basic difficulty in the formation and dissolution of the oedipus complex in a certain type of girl.

We have seen, in certain forms of infantilism, the result of a *disparity* in the development of ego and drive organization. While the development of the instinctual drives had been arrested and fixed at the oral stage, some ego functions had been brought to a higher level. The acceleration of ego development was partial; it led to high-level functioning, but only in certain areas: the parts of the ego that were not included in the process of precocious development remained at the level of the drive situation. It is not always clear whether this sort of precocious development is due to constitutional predisposition, or to environmental forces; apparently, both factors are involved.

In the cases I have analyzed, there has been evidence of a definite kind of pressure coming from the environment— more often, from the mothers. I am aware that every regression is, strictly speaking, infantile; in these cases, the developmental vicissitudes have resulted in the *entity* that I have called "infantilism."

Cases in which ego and superego development is accelerated, while drive development is slowed up, are familiar to us from the psychopathology of obsessional neuroses (Freud, Hartmann). That kind of acceleration has a defensive character; but the achievement of development in infantilism, as here described, has rather a compensatory function. These cases may sometimes impress us as being obsessional. For example, Betty's emotional life was quite ambivalent, yet her ambivalence could be traced to the emotional life of a child who had been arrested at the oral stage of development. Reactions of guilt may be quite strong, but they are not internalized, as they are in obsessional neuroses, and rather express fear of the loss of love and of the punishment that might come from the *external world*.

We have also mentioned the infantilism of girls in later adolescence, which is clearly in contrast with their often outstanding social and scholastic accomplishments. They seem not to be emotionally disturbed, as Betty was; I do not know many of them as analytic patients. Yet something in their behavior and appearance provides evidence of a discordance in their personalities. A young expectant mother, who is clad, in an advanced stage of her pregnancy, in little shorts; or a mature-looking freshman in miniskirts—these are familiar figures on college campuses. I am aware of difficulties in the maturation process before it reaches a state of definition, and before the adaptation to the social order in the role of "man" or "woman" has been achieved. Where there is no gross neurotic interference, further maturation will usually bring such developmental residue to a conclusion.

Infantilism, as the result of a certain developmental deficiency, is a well-known concept; it has attracted great attention and has found elaboration in analytic literature. Edith Jacobson (1964) has described pathological processes that are due to structural failures identical with those I have observed in adolescent girls.

I have perhaps devoted more attention to this topic than the aim of this study called for. But my observations on adolescent girls created in me the desire to introduce a *special entity,* which is expressed in a variety of clinical pictures. There have been attempts previously to create a clinical, well-defined unit, yet they have never been satisfactory. The fact that there is an incongruence in development between drives and ego, that there are partial developments that do not fully fit into the conception of infantilism, is probably responsible for the lack of complete clinical definition. The condition has thus not been established as a clinical entity; it has instead been considered to be a personality defect, met with in various clinical conditions, above all in hysteria.

OTHER TYPICAL PROBLEMS

In the assessment of the maturity of women, motherhood, or its psychological equivalent, is of great significance. I must emphasize that, according to my observations, girls—even during the early period of the adolescent process, and even in spite of great deficiencies in their psychic development—seem to behave, as a rule, in relation to reality, more maturely and more reliably than boys. Even in their still very juvenile approach to the other sex, they readily take the maternal role of helpers, protectors, providers. There is clearly an innate quality in action here!

Many problems face the modern adolescent girl. The most difficult, perhaps, is the girls' dual adolescent crisis: it is not only a search for identity as a mature woman; it is also a search for identity as a mother. The "progressive" ideology of equal rights for women often ignores the conflicts that arise as the result of these cultural changes. I am not now referring to problems of time and of home administration; there are deeper problems in regard to psychic energies and their distribution. Many young women in their late adolescence know and sometimes openly express their uncertainty about how to enjoy their new role in society and at the same time to be a full-time mother.

The main source of my information about the variety of problems in late adolescence, and specifically about those that face girls, was my consultations, in a procedure that I have described in Chapter 1 of this monograph. While the problems they came with were of a very personal nature, my patients had the character of members of a typical group.

I want now to present two cases, each of which was struggling with a problem that was quite typical of adolescence.

One of the girls, Nora, a nineteen-year-old sophomore in college, came to me to complain about her difficulties with boys. While she was still in high school, she used to have very devoted friendships with girls, all of whom she had left behind, she being the only one in the group to come to an Eastern college. She is quite popular with boys. As a matter of fact, it is not the lack of boys that causes the trouble; quite the contrary: she "goes" with *three* young men, and cannot decide which one to choose. When she is with Freddy, she feels that Johnny is the "one for her," or else it is David —and so forth. The boys are beginning to be impatient; she is afraid that time is passing, and she has not yet had a *real* love affair. As with many of my adolescent patients, there was no evidence of neurotic suffering, but rather a reality problem that Nora was not able to solve. Since she was an intuitive and not unsophisticated girl, however, she did not consider her problem to be purely one of reality.

All three of the boys concerned were directly connected with her high school past: two of them were brothers of her old girlfriends; the third had had a mild affair with another of her friends from back home. This information was sufficient for me to understand that the homosexual attachments of her earlier adolescence had not yet been fully resolved and had in fact continued into her present pseudoheterosexual relationships. I did not give Nora any intellectual counsel. I discussed with her the meaning that college held for her—how it was a step toward a kind of "new life," one that was more mature! We agreed that maintaining the emotional ties of her past and attaching them to her new experiences seemed to interfere with the excitement and surprises of her new college life. Apparently, my indirect advice fell on prepared ground. Nora began to have excuses when she was invited on a date with any one of the three hometown boys, and decided instead to meet a new one from somewhere else. This she did with success. Whether she then became aware of the role that had been played by her former girlfriends, I do not know. Anyhow, she is a clear example of the persistence of the early adolescent love for girls—especially when separation from the past milieu increased the longing for past attachments![4]

Another example is a girl whose complaints centered about her momentary difficulties with examinations—a problem that was more often brought to me by boys. Maria came from a highly intellectual family: her father was a college professor; three brothers were honor students, her mother a college graduate; Maria herself was a brilliant and very promising college junior. As the only girl in the family, she had always been her father's "pet," and she had never doubted her role in his life. Father would always assert, jokingly, that Maria,

---

[4] This inability to choose among a number of suitors, to sacrifice the others for the love of one, happens quite often during adolescence.

being the only one of her sex among his children, held a privileged position with him. He used to spend much of his time professionally in France and, back in America, dreamed of Paris; he promised Maria that, when she reached twenty, he would take her, during her summer vacation, to Paris *à deux,* and would show her all the wonders of French culture.

When I first met her, Maria was not looking forward to her trip with her father; instead, she was preoccupied with her spring term examinations. This was the first time that she had not been able to concentrate and to memorize; it was "as if my brains were not the same." Maria then told me her dreams. She even started her first interview with a dream of so manifestly a phallic character that I asked her whether she knew anything about dreams and their meaning; she replied that she did not.

As time went on, I understood her problem. Maria had become panicky as the time for the realization of her oedipal triumph approached. Paris had now become taboo for her, and all possible methods of defense had to be mobilized against it. If she was not able to complete her examinations in time, she would have to stay at home, in order to take summer courses (that was her conscious determination). She even attempted a compromise with herself: if she resigned her cherished role as the "only girl" in father's life, she might instead be able to go with him as one of his boys. Maria was apparently mobilizing the developmental residue of a "masculinity complex" in order to fulfill her wish to go to Paris as a boy. (The boyish attitude of girls in adolescence often has this same sort of defensive meaning.) Maria could not succeed as a boy, however, because she was too much her father's beloved girl and she wanted, in the end, to keep that position. But the voice of forbidding was stronger in her and it looked as though the dream of Paris would have to remain unrealized.

My interviews with Maria brought a very successful solution. The therapeutic approach was not very difficult for me:

I did not speak to Maria about her examinations, but about Paris, which I had loved so much in my adolescence that I could easily be the ally of her dreams. These conversations led to a conclusion that I communicated to Maria: "If I were you, I would say: 'To hell with the exams' and go to Paris!" Maria passed her examinations with honors and went off to Paris. In my rather uncomplicated handling of the situation, it was "grandmother's" *permission* that gave Maria the freedom to act that she needed!

Nora and Maria both reveal emotional problems that are typical of the adolescence of girls, and not only in our society. What makes them "contemporary" is the background of the psychological events: college life, inhibited activities with the opposite sex (Nora), and—especially with Maria—the conflict between her more feminine emotional involvements and the ambitions of a girl with "equal rights."

The psychological events observed here in individual cases can easily be expressed in terms of groups. I am of the opinion that the boyish attire of girls in their demonstrative activities may often represent—as with Maria—their oedipal struggles in a modern shape!

LATE ADOLESCENCE

Many girls—a great majority of them—outgrow, either in part or altogether, the confusions of contemporary youth. The life of those who do remain in a prolonged early adolescence assumes various forms. Some continue their primitive rebellion and fight for their "freedom," among them many intelligent and creative young people. Their creativity has diverse forms of expression, depending upon their particular talent. They go on living in protesting groups, except that these groups now have a more definite character. Some of the girls are visual artists of a specific "school," or else they continue the Beatle tradition in musical groups, smaller or larger. They often win mature audiences for themselves, and are an important part of the culture of our times. They were addicted to rhythm from the beginning in their "go! go!" and they continue this in the further development of their art into newer forms.

Some, to be sure, have nothing to offer society; they remain empty, confused rebels, until reality forces them into some degree of adjustment. In this respect, girls usually find their way to reality more easily and sooner than do boys. If they are not afflicted with infantilism, the rebellious attitude exhausts itself with their maturation. In their late adolescence, they look back, somewhat amused, to the period of their wild group activities. They were very much involved in those days in the process of identification with boys, sometimes with only one boy. Yet, even in their most aggressively wild activities, their femininity had been preserved in relationship to boys and had sometimes even proven dangerous in its masochistic component. In their later development, they may retreat to an individualistic way of life, very much under the influence of their home situation, or else join the boys in groups at a more mature, goal-directed social-political level. In college, this joining becomes to a certain degree automatic. The spirit in the dormitories of coeducational schools, as well as the housing arrangements, functions as "matchmakers" for group living, so that sexual relationships become a matter of course for these students.

In discussing adolescent boys, I referred to these dormitory groups, but I want to say something more with regard to the girls. Let us not forget that they too are functioning under the sign of "we" and its defensive role, and that conformity is also the main force among them. Sexuality plays a very important role here, and the "organization" is strictly a boy and a girl, in various multiples of two (usually eight). "Monogamy" is expected, at least "for the duration."

It may happen, however, that one of the pair—I know only about the girls in this respect—does not conform to the standards regarding sex. She is then considered abnormal—which gives me the opportunity to meet her. These are girls in their late teens or even early twenties, who do not feel ready for sexual experience. They wait for love, for sex without it holds no attraction for them. The sexual revolution is accepted by them as an intellectual conception, but they do not want their own sexual experience to take place at a time when they do not feel ready and mature enough for it. They accept from their peers the verdict of "abnormality," but with fear and sorrow, and they are extremely relieved when I reassure them about their normality.

This conservative attitude seems to be very common among our "modern" girls during their late adolescence, and I suspect that these limits are more determined by psychological and biological aspects than by sociological ones. As far as direct educational influences are in play, it is remarkable to learn that these girls often come to college with their mother's advice: "Be free sexually, but avoid pregnancy." My advice to postpone sexual experiences in terms of their own needs and wishes is often rejected; they are rather ashamed of their old-fashioned chastity, and prefer—if that is the actual choice —being considered "corrupt" to being known as "virginal."

To my surprise, I have not seen, as objects of direct observation, many girls in their late adolescence who were struggling with masculinity as a complex. I ascribe this to the fact that, at that moment of social development, the girls are absorbed by the possibility of sublimation: society presents them with a stage, on which they have the opportunity to fight and conquer! They are now in possession of the same social and cultural possibilities as boys and, in the fierce competition of this generation, a girl may aim at being the best among girls or merely enjoy the privilege of being in a society that sanctions competition with boys. For girls to be among the first ones on assignments that have until now been reserved for boys may have the same psychological significance for them as the "Nobel prize" has for boys.

In any case, one now hears complaints (seldom satisfaction) about the fact that girls are generally more ambitious, more ready to sacrifice other values of life for learning, memorizing and achieving grades, than boys are! There are indeed many female "Arnolds" among them!

The conflict between masculine and feminine, or between the new role in society and conservative emotional strivings, does not enter the field, as long as inhibitions and other difficulties that are rooted in these conflicts do not interfere. The majority of girls are able to keep these problems out of sight, often until they reach the immediate goal of their ambitions. Many drop out of college, in spite of good intellectual performances. Some of them look into the possibilities of marriage; some want to have jobs and participate in social activities (teaching, housing programs, etc.). After a while, it becomes clear that these girls have matured into womanhood and are fed up with being nothing more than ambitious schoolgirls. "Grades" and "brilliance" are no longer the highest goals in life for them.

Many continue their previous pursuits, especially when their choice of a man—whether it be in free love or in marriage—is built on a community of intellectual, professional, and social interests. In European countries, such marriages used to be called a "community of desks," instead of a "community of beds."

Conflict arises when pregnancy—wanted or not wanted—interferes with the attainment of previous goals, or when giving birth to a child creates a change of emotional atmosphere in the women. In these cases, the still persisting process of late adolescence changes its character. Motherhood may be an important factor in the consolidation of maturity; it may also, however, be a trauma, with various consequences. We must not forget the role of the father, who reacts to this new complication in terms of his own personality. He may still be in need of a desk companion, or of an active mother substitute, such as his girlfriend (wife) had been until now for him.

We are here involved with a very serious problem, which

goes beyond the framework of this writing. In the light of the expressions of increased public interest, as well as the great efforts being made by educational forces toward the solution of this problem, one gets the impression of an acute and alarming development. Yet the problems are exactly the same as they were three generations earlier, in old European countries, if one considers them in relation to individual women. The social changes since then; the actual participation of women in all those aspects of life that had previously been reserved for men; equality in education, etc.—it is these things that have transformed the question into a mass problem, and correspondingly shifted its solution from the psychological to the sociological field.

Attempts to investigate the core of the problem—the girls' attitude toward the conflicts created by motherhood—must, by the very nature of the approach I have indicated, remain at a comparatively superficial level. Whether the girl declares a greater interest in intellectual pursuits and a career, or in marriage and motherhood, depends upon the state of mind she is in at the time of the inquiry, the actual influence of her most immediate milieu, the personality of her boyfriend, etc. Since my dealing with these problems is not as a professional investigator, the information I obtain is much less under the control of the intellect.

Many girls plan for both profession and family, completely unaware of the fact that there exists a deep and powerful conflict of emotional energy (libido), a problem of the disposition of that inner energy that cannot serve one goal without being drawn away from the other. Their intuitive feeling may create in some of them the legitimate anxiety that such a conflict of interests may arise. But it is only through personal experience that they come to acknowledge fully the existence of the psychological problems involved. Social milieu, of course, the cultural values of the environment, are of great importance. But the solution lies less in society than it does in the individual's capacity. Society is able to help by external arrangements—which do not really solve the problem. Even the arrangements that have been made in Russia and in Israel, which are probably the best of their kind, are not solutions. Motherhood is a tyrannical full-time emotional task; part-time motherhood is a compromise that hurts both masters: professional work and motherhood.

There are women who, through their unusual gifts and their capacity to adjust, seem to have fulfilled both tasks successfully. I have been happy to know them, and have often referred to them as good examples in support of my belief that the conflict can be solved. In a number of cases, however, I have been able to obtain some insight into the adolescence of their children. The shock of these revelations has led me definitely to give up my optimistic view.

Where opinions and observations are in direct opposition to one another, and the responses of those who are under consideration—"modern women"—are vacillating and in search of compromises, one cannot help feeling that only time and further developments will bring any general answer to the problem. Until then, the solution must remain individual: each "case" the master of its own decision!

BIBLIOGRAPHY

Benedek, T. (1959), Parenthood as a Developmental Phase: A Contribution to the Libido Theory. *J. Amer. Psychoanal. Assn.*, 8:389-417.

Bernfeld, S. (1924), *Vom Dichterischen Schaffen der Jugend.* Vienna: Internationaler Psychoanalytischer Verlag.

——— (1938), Types of Adolescence. *Psychoanal. Quart.*, 7:243-253.

Bibring, G. L. (1959), Some Considerations of the Psychological Processes in Pregnancy. *The Psychoanalytic Study of the Child*, 14:113-121. New York: International Universities Press.

Blair, G. B., Jr. (1966), *Youth and the Hazards of Affluence.* New York: Harper & Row.

Blos, P. (1954), Prolonged Adolescence: The Formulation of a Syndrome and Its Therapeutic Implications. *Amer. J. Orthopsychiat.*, 24:733-742.

——— (1958), Preadolescent Drive Organization. *J. Amer. Psychoanal. Assn.*, 6:47-56.

——— (1962), *On Adolescence: A Psychoanalytic Interpretation.* New York: Free Press of Glencoe.

Brunswick, R. M. (1940), The Preoedipal Phase of Libido Development. *Psychoanal. Quart.*, 9:293-319.

Deutsch, F. (1959), Creative Passion of the Artist and Its Synesthetic Aspects. *Int. J. Psycho-Anal.*, 40:38-51.

Deutsch, H. (1932), On Female Homosexuality. *Psychoanal. Quart.*, 1:484-510.

——— (1937a), Don Quixote and Don Quixotism. *Neuroses and Character Types.* New York: International Universities Press, 1965, pp. 218-225.

——— (1937b), Absence of Grief. *Neuroses and Character Types.* New York: International Universities Press, 1965, pp. 226-236.

——— (1939), A Discussion of Certain Forms of Resistance. *Neuroses and Character Types.* New York: International Universities Press, 1965, pp. 248-261.

131

—— (1942), Some Forms of Emotional Disturbances and Their Relationship to Schizophrenia. *Neuroses and Character Types*. New York: International Universities Press, 1965, pp. 262-286.

—— (1944), *The Psychology of Women:* Vol. 1. *Girlhood*. New York: Grune & Stratton.

—— (1945), *The Psychology of Women:* Vol. 2. *Motherhood*. New York: Grune & Stratton.

—— (1964), Some Clinical Considerations of the Ego Ideal. *J. Amer. Psychoanal. Assn.*, 12:512-516.

Dodds, E. R. (1951), *The Greeks and the Irrational*. Berkeley: University of California Press.

Eissler, K. R. (1958), Notes on Problems of Technique in the Psychoanalytic Treat of Adolescents: With Some Remarks on Perversions. *The Psychoanalytic Study of the Child*, 13:223-254. New York: International Universities Press.

—— (1963), *Goethe: A Psychoanalytic Study*. Detroit: Wayne University Press.

Erikson, E. H. (1950), *Childhood and Society*. New York: W. W. Norton.

—— (1956), The Problem of Ego Identity. *J. Amer. Psychoanal. Assn.*, 4:56-121.

—— (1958), *Young Man Luther: A Study in Psychoanalysis and History*. New York: W. W. Norton.

Fraiberg, S. (1955), Some Considerations in the Introduction to Therapy in Puberty. *The Psychoanalytic Study of the Child*, 10:264-286. New York: International Universities Press.

Freud, A. (1936), *The Ego and the Mechanisms of Defense*. New York: International Universities Press, rev. ed., 1966.

—— (1958), Adolescence. *The Psychoanalytic Study of the Child*, 13:255-278. New York: International Universities Press.

Freud, S. (1873), Letter to E. Fluss. In: *Letters of Sigmund Freud*, ed. E. Freud. New York: Basic Books, 1960, pp. 3-6.

—— (1908), Hysterical Phantasies and Their Relation to Bisexuality. *Standard Edition*, 9:155-166. London: Hogarth Press, 1959.

—— (1914), On Narcissism: An Introduction. *Standard Edition*, 14:73-102. London: Hogarth Press, 1957.

—— (1920), Beyond the Pleasure Principle. *Standard Edition:* 18:3-64. London: Hogarth Press, 1955.

—— (1921), Group Psychology and the Analysis of the Ego. *Standard Edition*, 18:69-143. London: Hogarth Press, 1955.

—— (1927), The Future of an Illusion. *Standard Edition*, 21:5-56. London: Hogarth Press, 1961.

—— (1930), Civilization and Its Discontents. *Standard Edition*, 21:57-145. London: Hogarth Press, 1961.

—— (1933 [1932]), New Introductory Lectures on Psycho-Analysis. *Standard Edition*, 22:3-182. London: Hogarth Press, 1964.

Friedenberg, E. Z. (1959), *The Vanishing Adolescent*. Boston: Beacon Press.

────── (1965a) *Coming of Age in America: Growth and Acquiescence*. New York: Random House.

────── (1965b), *The Dignity of Youth and Other Atavisms*. Boston: Beacon Press.

Geleerd, E. (1961), Some Aspects of Ego Vicissitudes in Adolescence. *J. Amer. Psychoanal. Assn.,* 9:394-405.

Greenacre, P. (1957), The Childhood of the Artist. *The Psychoanalytic Study of the Child,* 12:47-72.

────── (1962), The Early Years of the Gifted Child: A Psychoanalytic Interpretation. In: *Year Book of Education,* ed. G. Z. F. Bereday & J. A. Lauwerys. London: Evans Brothers, pp. 71-90.

Hartmann, H. (1944), Psychoanalysis and Sociology. *Essays in Ego Psychology.* New York: International Universities Press, 1964, pp. 19-36.

────── (1955), Notes on the Theory of Sublimation. *The Psychoanalytic Study of the Child,* 10:9-29. New York: International Universities Press.

────── (1964), *Essays in Ego Psychology: Selected Problems in Psychoanalytic Theory.* New York: International Universities Press.

Hitschmann, E. (1956), *Great Men: Psychoanalytic Studies.* New York: International Universities Press.

Jacobson, E. (1961), Adolescent Moods and the Remodeling of Psychic Structures in Adolescence. *The Psychoanalytic Study of the Child,* 16:164-183. New York: International Universities Press.

────── (1964), *The Self and the Object World.* New York: International Universities Press.

Katan, M. (1954), The Importance of the Non-Psychotic Part of the Personality in Schizophrenia. *Int. J. Psycho-Anal.,* 35:119-128.

────── (1958), Contribution to the Panel on Ego-Distortion. *Int. J. Psycho-Anal.,* 39:265-270.

Katz, J. (1965), Quoted by J. Michalak: Campus Conformity Reported. *Boston Globe,* October 8, 1965.

Kazantzakis, N. (1965), *Report to Greco.* New York: Simon & Schuster.

Keniston, K. (1965), *The Uncommitted: Alienated Youth in American Society.* New York: Harcourt, Brace & World.

Kerenyi, C. (1951), *The Gods of the Greeks.* London, New York: Thames & Hudson.

Kohut, H. (1966), Forms and Transformations of Narcissism. *J. Amer. Psychoanal. Assn.,* 14:243-272.

Kris, E. (1952), *Psychoanalytic Explorations in Art.* New York: International Universities Press.

Lampl-de Groot, J. (1960), On Adolescence. *The Psychoanalytic Study of the Child,* 15:95-103. New York: International Universities Press.

Laufer, M. (1964), Ego Ideal and Pseudo Ego Ideal in Adolescence. *The Psychoanalytic Study of the Child,* 19:196-221. New York: International Universities Press.

——— (1965), Assessment of Adolescent Disturbances: The Application of Anna Freud's Diagnostic Profile. *The Psychoanalytic Study of the Child,* 20:99-123. New York: International Universities Press.

Loomie, L. S., Rosen, V. H., & Stein, M. H. (1958), Ernst Kris and the Gifted Adolescent Project. *The Psychoanalytic Study of the Child,* 13:44-63. New York: International Universities Press.

Lorand, S. & Schneer, H. I., eds. (1965), *Adolescents.* New York: Hoeber.

Miller, M. V. & Gilmore, S., eds. (1965), *Revolution in Berkeley: The Crisis in American Education.* New York: Dell Publishing Co.

Murray, J. M. (1964), Narcissism and the Ego Ideal. *J. Amer. Psychoanal.* Assn., 12:477-511.

Parsons, T. (1964), *Social Structure and Personality.* New York: Free Press of Glencoe.

Rexford, E. N., ed. (1966), *A Developmental Approach to Problems of Acting Out* [Journal of the American Academy of Child Psychiatry, Monogr. 1]. New York: International Universities Press.

Riesman, D. (1950), *The Lonely Crowd: A Study of the Changing American Character.* New Haven: Yale University Press.

Rochlin, G. (1965), *Griefs and Discontents: The Forces of Change.* Boston: Little, Brown.

Schiff, L. (1964), The Obedient Rebels: A Study of College Conversions to Conservatism. *J. Social Issues,* 20:74-95.

Spiegel, L. A. (1951), A Review of Contributions to a Psychoanalytic Theory of Adolescence. *The Psychoanalytic Study of the Child,* 6:375-393. New York: International Universities Press.

——— (1958), Comments on the Psychoanalytic Psychology of Adolescence. *The Psychoanalytic Study of the Child,* 13:296-308. New York: International Universities Press.

Tartakoff, H. (1966), The Normal Personality in Our Culture and the Nobel Prize Complex. In: *Psychoanalysis—A General Psychology: Essays in Honor of Heinz Hartmann,* ed. R. M. Loewenstein, L. M. Newman, M. Schur, & A. J. Solnit. New York: International Universities Press, pp. 222-252.

Waelder, R. (1924), Über Mechanismen und Beeinflussungsmöglichkeiten der Psychosen. *Int. Z. Psychoanal.,* 10:393-414.

Wiener, N. (1953), *Ex-Prodigy: My Childhood and Youth.* New York: Simon & Schuster.

Zborowski, M. & Herzog, E. (1952), *Life Is with People.* New York: International Universities Press.

ABOUT THE AUTHOR

HELENE DEUTSCH received her M.D. in 1912 from the University of Vienna and subsequently underwent psychoanalysis with Sigmund Freud. She became a member of the Vienna Psychoanalytic Society in 1918. In 1925 she became Director of the Vienna Psychoanalytic Institute, a position she maintained until her departure for the United States in 1935. In 1937 she became a permanent member of the Boston Psychoanalytic Society and Institute and has been on the faculty ever since. In 1962 she received the Charles Frederick Menninger Award for her epochal contributions to psychoanalysis. She is Honorary Professor at Boston University and a staff member of the Massachusetts General Hospital.

Among Dr. Deutsch's publications are *Psychoanalysis of the Neuroses* (1930), the two-volume *Psychology of Women* (1944-1945), and *Neuroses and Character Types* (1965), which includes her first book as well as her most important papers.

Dr. Deutsch has used her partial retirement to engage in a study of contemporary adolescents, an unorthodox investigation resulting in the present monograph.